Taking the Piss

A Potted History of Pee

ADAM HART-DAVIS
& EMILY TROSCIANKO

Taking the Piss
A Potted
History
of Pee

With illustrations by

JOLYON TROSCIANKO

THE
CHALFORD
PRESS

First published 2006

The Chalford Press
The Mill, Brimscombe Port, Stroud, Gloucestershire, GL5 2QG
www.tempus-publishing.com

The Chalford Press is an imprint of NPI Media Group Limited

British Library Cataloguing in Publication Data.
A catalogue record for this book is available from the British Library.

ISBN 1 84588 351 9
ISBN-13 (from January 2007) 978 1 84588 351 5

Printed in Great Britain by Oaklands Book Services Limited

Contents

Foreword

As an eleven-year-old boy with a Kevin Keegan haircut, I had dreams of standing on the steps of Wembley Stadium, holding aloft the FA Cup. So when, thirty years later, I found myself on the stage at the Royal Society, holding an award for making a radio programme about human urine recycling, I knew that my career wasn't going according to plan.

It all began when my five-year-old daughter noticed a bad smell as we drove past a sewerage works. She was incredulous at my attempts to explain what happens to human waste, and, as an archaeologist, my wife then chipped in with her short history of how useful urine was before we decided it was just so much filth. A couple of phone calls later and I had what resembled a programme idea to take to Radio 4.

The powers-that-be took some convincing that listeners actually wanted to know how urine had been used in the past, but I had one final, compelling card to play. My programme would be presented by Adam Hart-Davis, probably the only man in the country who could make such a subject sound nothing short of fascinating without lapsing into the occasional bout of toilet humour.

Adam has the sort of frightening enthusiasm for science that makes you wish you had paid attention at school. A devotee of the exploits of Thomas Crapper, Adam's knowledge of our chosen specialist subject made producing it a piece of … cake.

Our story began in Adam's back garden, where his straw urinal offered a modest but practical place to contemplate why the chemical components of urine make it a very useful commodity.

From the Romans brushing their teeth with urine to the demands of the twentieth-century textile industry and all stops in between, we discovered how urine has been used by chemists, medics, farmers, soldiers and industrialists. And, after discovering that the Romans collected urine in piss pots in the street, it was reassuring to find that a character with the highly appropriate name of Piss Willy was still doing this in the villages of North Yorkshire in the 1930s.

The title of the programme – *Taking the Piss out of London* – was, admittedly, rather misleading from a listener's point-of-view. Perhaps someone did tune in hoping to hear a clutch of malcontented provincial comics sneering at the self-importance of our capital city. But, within minutes, Adam's affectionate and vivid description of his straw urinal would have convinced them that this was a very different proposition.

The title refers to one possible source of the phrase 'taking the piss.' Apparently, some sea captains taking urine up the east coast of England to supply Yorkshire's eighteenth-century alum industry were not very proud of their down-market cargo. To boost their low self-esteem, they would pretend to be carrying wine, only to face the retort, 'Go on, you're taking the piss!'

And the award? Well, the programme went down very well, and has been known to get the occasional rerun on the network which, given its recycling theme, is only fitting. The Association of British Science Writers gave us the award for making the science readily accessible and entertaining, and it now hangs on my wall – in the lavatory.

John Byrne
Producer, BBC Radio 4
20 March 2005

Introduction and Acknowledgements

Nine years ago Adam offered a publisher a quartet of reference books – *EncycLOOpedia*, *EncycloPOOdia*, *EncycloPEEdia*, and *Enfarta* – but they turned him down, and all that came out was a little book about lavatories, called *Thunder, Flush, and Thomas Crapper*. It would have been longer, but the editor was ruthless, and insisted on cutting the crap.

Seven years later, radio producer John Byrne, champion of wacky ideas, suggested we should make a radio programme called *Taking the Piss out of London*. We did, and it won an award, and a publisher then asked whether there could be a book about it. Luckily, Adam had both his old files and an enthusiastic co-author, and we set to work. There turns out to be a mountain – or perhaps a lake – of material about urine, just waiting to be sucked up. Peeing is such a routine function in life that people have not only found weird and wonderful ways and places to do it, and a plethora of uses for the stuff, but have also written about it extensively, and used urine in every medium of art. This is not a comprehensive account – we have left out more than we could cram in – but we hope it is an enjoyable taster.

We would like to acknowledge help in the research from Katherine Birkett, Roland Clare and The Beanstalk, Simon

Rose, Joanna Warham, Matthew Whitfield and others, while John Byrne discovered Jennifer Stead's useful paper on 'The Uses of Urine' in *Old West Riding*.

Adam Hart-Davis
Emily Troscianko
August 2006

One

Why We Wee

Urine is about ninety-five per cent water; so 'passing water' is a sensible euphemism for urinating. In addition it contains urea, uric acid, a trace of amino acids and some salts, which are all waste materials that need to be flushed out of the body.

There is also a dash of chemicals called urobilins, which used to be called urochrome, and are what makes urine yellow; they are closely related to bilirubin, which is responsible for the brown colour of faeces. When it is concentrated, in the morning, for example, the colour is darker yellow, and may even be brownish; when the urine is more dilute – after you have drunk a lot of liquid – the urine is paler.

The element nitrogen is an important part of all amino acids, which are the building blocks of proteins. We need to eat proteins to build and repair muscles and other bodily tissues, and we get them from pulses, dairy products, eggs, fish and meat. The body breaks down the incoming protein into amino acids, and uses them to build the proteins it needs, and there is always some left over. We need to get rid of the excess, and in particular the nitrogen, which can otherwise cause problems.

One of the simplest compounds of nitrogen is ammonia, but this is seriously poisonous; our livers, therefore, make a more complex compound, urea, which is soluble in water and can be stored safely until we are ready to pee it out. The urea is passed in the blood to the kidneys, from where a watery solution is pumped to the bladder and – when we are ready – to the urethra for peeing.

Urea was the first 'organic' compound to be made in the laboratory. In 1828 a German chemist, Friedrich Wohler, was using ordinary lab chemicals to try to make ammonium cyanate, but what he actually made was urea. He was so excited that he wrote to a colleague, 'I must tell you that I can make urea without the use of kidneys, either man or dog. Ammonium cyanate is urea.' Until then people had generally believed that all organic compounds contained some 'vital force' that was special for living things. Wohler's synthesis made it clear that urea, at least, was just an ordinary chemical.

Fish don't bother to make urea. They just let the surplus nitrogen form ammonia, which is immensely soluble in water and is flushed out of the system via the gills as the fish swims. Birds, by contrast, can't afford to carry around as much water as land animals, so they turn the nitrogen into the solid uric acid. That is why most bird poo is at least partly white – the white part is the uric acid, the bird equivalent of urine.

In general we feel we want to wee when the bladder is full, and it fills more quickly when we drink more liquid. Beer in particular makes you pee more, both because of its volume and because it is mildly diuretic. Diuretics are substances that increase the production of urine. Doctors often prescribe what they coyly call 'water pills', which come with such complicated chemical names as indapamide hemihydrate, but there are plenty of natural diuretics, including coffee, tea, green tea, and honey, and the vegetables asparagus, celery, parsley, dandelion leaves and stinging nettles.

People have a tendency to think of urine as 'dirty', but in practice it is remarkably clean. Unless you have an infection of the bladder or urethra, your urine will be sterile, and slightly bactericidal. In many cultures it has been used for washing and cleaning wounds – much safer than unpurified water. Some people believe in drinking their urine, and even assert that it can be good for your health, as we will look at more closely in Chapter Four.

Two

Where We Wee

Historically, most people have simply gone to pee in the open – in the bush, in the river, or behind any convenient structure. In many parts of developing countries this is still the case, and it poses a worrying problem for girls. Often they will not go to school unless there are good latrines there; and even at home they will often wait in growing discomfort, until it is dark enough for them to slip out to the bush – where they are in danger of being attacked by animals or men.

The latrine or privy provides a private place to pee. Traditionally a privy was just a wooden hut, with a seat over a hole in the ground. Sometimes earth from the hole would be used to cover each offering. Paper was often provided in the form of newspaper torn into small squares and hung on a nail. Americans traditionally used pages of the Sears catalogue, which also made good reading matter.

The oldest-known lavatories in the world are at Skara Brae on Orkney, where a 5,000-year-old stone-age settlement of some eight houses was uncovered in 1850. Each one-room house has a little alcove with a hole in the middle of the floor. The holes lead down into drains that run beneath all the houses and down towards the sea.

The Romans brought efficient flushing lavatories to Britain, and the remains of one communal loo can be seen at Housesteads on Hadrian's Wall. After the Romans left, we seem to have ignored their sanitary example, and water closets did not reappear for several hundred years. Indeed, not until the middle of the nineteenth century did most houses in Britain acquire piped water and a water-closet, and even then many were in outside privies.

No one enjoyed going out to the privy in the middle of the night, so in case you wanted to pee you would keep a chamber pot under the bed. Some people called the pot a gozunder – because it goes under the bed. Chamber pots came in many shapes and sizes: for rich people they might be of pewter or even silver, but most were made of glazed porcelain. Some were beautifully decorated; some had portraits of Hitler or other hate-figures that you might enjoy pissing on. Two hundred years earlier the target was Dr Henry Sachaverell, a radical preacher and politician. The potter who had the idea of making the Sachaverell pots made a fortune and built himself a huge house, which was known locally as Piss-Pot Hall.

In Victorian times pots were often printed with jokes and vulgar rhymes. Some had a picture of an eye looking up, with the lines 'Use me well and keep me clean,/And I'll not tell what I have seen.'

Glass pee-bottles with wide necks were sometimes called jordans or looking-glasses, and were used by doctors for diagnosis (see page 55). In hospitals today men who have trouble getting out of bed are provided with disposable pee-bottles made from recycled paper. Women have to be helped on to bedpans, which is less comfortable.

Men generally pee while standing. In public lavatories, including those in restaurants and shops, men are usually provided with urinals (pronounced YOURinals or yeRINE-als), so that they can stand up to pee. This has long been a cause of contention. At the Great Exhibition of 1851, the women who wanted to pee in the public lavatories in the Crystal Palace had to spend a penny to do so (see page 100), while the men were able to use the urinals for free. The same discrepancy has occurred in countless places since then. Often today in theatres and cinemas there are the same numbers of cubicles for women as there are urinals for men. Since it takes women roughly twice as long as men to perform – they have to go into a cubicle, remove clothing, and sit down – there should be twice as many loos for women as for men. In practice, there never are, and there is always a queue outside the Ladies'.

Various inventors have tried to solve this problem, by making urinals for women – some to be used facing the wall and some facing out. They are generally low and without a seat; the women squat above the pan. An early model was the 1927 urinette, situated in a cubicle, with a curtain across the front. The urinette was tried in thirty places in London, but the subsequent report said they 'are not popular … They are sometimes used in an unclean fashion, and require supervision to maintain them in a hygienic condition.' In other words, they ran into the fact that men are taught from an early age to pee standing up and to poo sitting down, while women are not taught to separate the two separate excretory processes; they tend to sit down and just let go.

Because men generally prefer to pee standing there can be difficulties in the home if they pee on the lavatory seat: 'If you sprinkle when you tinkle, be a sweet and wipe the seat.' Women complain that men don't bother to raise the seat, or don't bother to put it down again. All sorts of inventions have tried to bridge this gap, from traffic lights to warn of a raised seat to automatic seats that spring up when a sitting user rises. In schools, the answer was often the divided seat – a fixed wooden seat with a gap in the front.

Peeing on the Move

Peeing gets more complicated when you are caught short out in the open. In the country, men can usually find a convenient tree or hut to pee behind, but in town there are real problems at night. Men come out of bars full of beer and unload it against buildings, which get smelly and stained. One solution is the pop-up urinal that now appears in the centres of many cities in Europe. Council officials use remote controls to summon them out of the ground in the early evening, and men seem quite happy to pee there in public. No solution for women.

Women used to do better, however, in seventeenth-century France, where the church services were desperately long. They used to take in pee-bottles and use them discreetly under their voluminous dresses (see also page 88). The bottles became known as bordaloues, in honour of a Jesuit priest, Louis Bordaloue, whose sermons were famously bladder-straining.

In modern Bangkok you can easily be stuck in traffic jams for five or six hours. A specially designed pee-bottle, the Comfort 100, solved the problem for men. A new device called the Indipod is described as a portable chemical unit with a nylon cubicle, which is inflated by a fan plugged into the cigarette lighter; it does sound as though to use this you would need not only a large car, but twenty minutes on the hard shoulder.

One solution for the woman on the move is a funnel that fits the female underneath and allows women to pee while standing up, and through gaps in clothing. Women who use them say they are marvellous when out hiking, jogging, canoeing, skiing, or at festivals. With care and some wriggling they can be used in a car, although not while driving. There are many funnels available, including the whiz (www.whizaway. com), the urinelle (www.urinelle.biz) and the p-mate (www. p-mate.com), not to mention the Pee-Zee, the TravelMate, the Freshette and the Whizzy. One disadvantage is that women have learned from an early age to pee sitting down, and psychologically many find it extremely difficult to pee while standing up. However, patience and practice usually prevail, and there is even a book, by Anna Skinner, called *How to Pee Standing Up – Tips for Hip Chicks*.

People in small boats generally use the 'bucket and chuck it' method – as did Dame Ellen MacArthur when she sailed alone round the world in a record-breaking seventy-one days in her not-so-small twenty-three-metre trimaran. Cyclists in races don't stop at all, and cycling shorts are thin and non-absorbent; so do not ride close up behind another cyclist in a long race.

Astronauts in recent years have used NASA's Waste Collection System, which is rather like a throne on which the users can strap themselves down, to avoid floating away at an awkward moment. Urine is collected by suction through a rubber hose with a soft rubber nozzle on the end. This nozzle was designed to fit astronauts of either sex, and as a result fits neither very well. Furthermore, the vacuum is never quite strong enough, so that the nozzle always seems to be wet from the last user.

WCS users, however, are lucky compared to the first American astronaut, Alan Sheppard, who was zipped into a skin-tight space suit and launched from Cape Canaveral on 5 May 1961. He was lying on his back in a foetal position, with minimal space for moving his arms and legs, and a steel plate in front of his face where there should have been a window. The flight was due to last only 15 minutes, so there were no lavatorial facilities. However, the countdown was repeatedly delayed until he had been waiting in the capsule for four hours, and had to pee. 'Go in the suit' he was told, and so he did. The warm urine trickled around his waist and collected under the small of his back, leaving Sheppard, the pioneer of American spaceflight, to be blasted into space lying in a cooling pool of his own piss.

NASA realized after this that they had to do something about what they called 'waste management', and the next groups of astronauts were provided with 'intimate-contact devices': they peed into a 'roll-on cuff-and-bag system' and crapped into 'absorbent diaper-type underwear and a stick-on colostomy bag'.

Similar systems are used by RAF fighter pilots today. Sitting in a Harrier, for example, you are hemmed in by your seat and the instruments, and cannot move more than a couple of inches

ZERO GRAVITY TOILET INSTRUCTIONS

in any direction. Male pilots use a 'Bag, aircrew relief,' commonly known as a piss bag, which is a transparent plastic bag, one-third the size of a hot-water bottle, with a one-way valve at the top and a sponge inside to stop the pee sloshing about. This is reasonably easy to use if you are wearing only a flying suit, but if you are fully togged up in a goon bag (Aircrew dry suit) you have to get through a 5-inch zip in the crotch, unroll the fitted 4.5-inch tube, push aside the g-suit (like a corset), unzip the flying suit and then penetrate thermals and underpants. This tricky operation requires both hands, so first you have to disable the ejection seat, and second you have to engage the autopilot, which will keep you at a steady altitude. Female pilots, we understand, wear nappies inside their flying suits.

In earlier days, and in larger aircraft, the pilot often had a leather bottle clipped to the fuselage beside his seat. Other members of the crew used a rubber hose that passed through the fuselage and into the air outside, which worked well unless the aircrew had annoyed the ground crew, when they might discover too late that the rubber tube had a knot in it. Large aircraft had an actual chemical lavatory – so when the Dam Busters went, they went on Elsans.

Three

Emergencies

Gas Masks

Poison gas killed an uncertain number of soldiers in the First World War, but it was almost certainly the weapon they most feared; at least death by machine gun was more likely to be instant, where gas could bring days or even weeks of agony. The first gas, used by the French in 1914, was xylyl bromide, in grenade form, more an irritant than a killer; the Germans responded with gas shells that caused violent sneezing fits but, again, only incapacitated for temporary advantage. The first true poison gas – chlorine – was released by the Germans using artillery shells at the Second Battle of Ypres in April 1915. The British response, using gas cylinders, at Loos in September, ended in disaster as the wind changed and the gas blew back on to those who had unloosed it. Chlorine was succeeded by phosgene and mustard gas – the former was particularly pernicious through an action delayed until it was already embedded and ineradicable, the latter so devastating because it more quickly caused external and internal blisters and blindness.

The first recommendations for defence against poison gas were that soldiers protect themselves using cloths moistened with urine, or earth folded in cloth or enclosed in a bottle with its base removed. A month later, the troops were equipped with double layers of flannel dipped in a sodium hydroxide solution kept in bottles in the trenches, though when they were caught out in the open, urine was still the only option. Eventually the men were issued with gas masks, but almost as crucial as those original helmets' effectiveness was the psychological sense they combated that their wearers were being left out for slaughter – a feeling which must have been overpowering in that first panicked pissing on a piece of rag.

Army Rations

The masterminds behind the 'indestructible sandwich' with a three-year life-span have given the US military an even weirder and more wonderful foodstuff: dried rations that troops can hydrate using water from the murkiest puddle – or their own urine. The Combat Feeding Directorate assures the soldiers that the filter in the pouch which holds the dried food removes 99.9% of the bacteria, and most of the toxic chemicals, from the liquid used to rehydrate it.

The filter works by osmosis: when two solutions of different concentrations are separated by a semipermeable membrane – one with gaps through which only water molecules will pass – the water is drawn to the more concentrated side. This particular membrane is a thin sheet of a cellulose-based plastic, its fibres half a nanometre apart – a gap too small for a bacterium to squeeze through.

The hungry soldier pees into one end of a foil sachet which contains two inner pouches separated by this membrane, and the water from the piss seeps through the membrane into the dehydrated food on the other side. A highly concentrated solution is created, as large molecules in the food are dissolved by the water, and the resulting osmotic pressure in turn draws more water through, till the food is as moist and succulent as it's going to get – first up on the experimental menu is chicken and rice.

This technology allows the weight of a three-meal daily ration to be reduced from 3.5 kilograms to about 0.4 – but the makers of the membrane stress that urine should remain the emergency option, because the membrane is too coarse to filter out urea; although urea is non-toxic in small amounts, to use this method over a longer period would cause kidney damage. Nonetheless, the knowledge that deep in some Middle Eastern desert one's own bladder could be the well-spring from which a delectable feast will mushroom, mirage-like but satiating, must be more consoling than the possibility of staving off dehydration with unmediated piss.

Drinking

Although millions swear by the benefits of making urine-drinking part of everyday life, to be forced to it by thirst is a different matter. The taste can range from utterly disgusting to simply odd – though one's own is said to be usually better than someone else's. Fresh is better than stale; some pee is highly alkaline, but most is mild and slightly salty; certain foods, such as garlic and asparagus, beans and peanuts, meat, milk and eggs, can make the smell and taste highly unpleasant. And drinking too little water (the reason for resorting to emergency urine-drinking in the first place) concentrates the urine, intensifying scent and flavour, usually disagreeably – until in the end it runs out, dries up entirely, concentrated and recycled out of existence: man cannot live by urine alone.

Although urine itself is sterile, it can pick up a variety of bacteria as it leaves the body through unwashed or infected genitalia – the precaution of washing the area before drinking (and collecting the liquid in mid-stream) is one that might be open to sailors, but not to desert-wanderers, delirious with thirst. Moreover, any tiny abrasions or tears on the lips or in the mouth, almost inevitable in the parched and chapped skin of the emergency urine-drinker, increase the danger of bacteria entering the bloodstream.

Other more minor crises than life-threatening thirst might have urine as their solution, as an inner source of warmth rather than of liquid: to free a frozen tongue from a metal pole (it does happen beyond the silver screen – the flagpole scene in the 1983 film *A Christmas Story* seems itself to have spawned a slew of children's imitations, as painful as their inspiration promises), to warm a cyclist's hands, to de-ice a windscreen or a car door lock …

Four

Health

Urotherapy/Uropathy

Urine's crude quality as a mere liquid, to which all its ingredients but water are simply impurities, makes it an emergency cure for dehydration; but these very impurities are what many hold up as the qualities of an elixir. In the simplest cases, it is a source of nutrients which are otherwise in short supply – in extreme climates, for example, salt, magnesium, calcium, potassium, vitamin C and various B vitamins – and may taste positively delicious as a result of the body's cravings.

Beyond the correction of temporary imbalances or deficiencies, though, a glass a day to keep the doctor away has its advocates the world over. One estimate in 2001 reported three million Chinese devotees of the daily tonic, most prizing in particular the first pee of the day, believing that because the body at rest requires fewer nutrients than the daytime body, the unused excess is released on rising – to be gleefully harnessed by the wise for the rigours of the day to come.

Preachers of urine's biochemical wonders proclaim a litany of vitamins, minerals, proteins, enzymes, hormones, antibodies and amino acids, running into the thousands; among the most wondrous, DHEA (the steroid to which are attributed anti-ageing and anti-cancer miracles), allantoin (to promote wound-healing), factor S (to induce sleep), gastric secretory depressants (to combat ulcer growth), urokinase (to dissolve blood clots) and, of course, urea (a major part of many antibacterial substances); some even claim that uric acid may be at the root of human longevity relative to other mammals. Nonetheless, in the West, pee-drinking remains strictly for the bohemian and the desperate, those familiar with Eastern philosophies such as Hinduism and Taoism (see Superstition and Spirituality) and those seeking to prolong life or improve health, be it physical or spiritual.

While most people think of urine as a waste product, urinophiles claim that it is the scientifically-minded sceptics who are themselves being misled – by the big business that converts urokinase, for example, into acceptable tablets: dissolving blood clots all over the Western world, but keeping quiet about the limitless nectar that could dissolve their profits if pill-popping gave way to piss-swigging. UT (urine therapy) enthusiasts remind us that if we are too squeamish to drink our own piss, we should be squeamish, too, about some of the little white pills we eat, since their ingredients have to come from somewhere – and they come, amongst other sources, from those porta-loos ubiquitous at festivals and concerts, filled with the stench of chemicals and all that quickly converted beer.

The American company Porta-John, a subsidiary of Enzymes of America Holding Corp., in collaboration with Pharmaceuticals.org, Inc, features a special filter for collecting the pee proteins; the partnership has, as their website proudly proclaims, 'been developing methods of harvesting human generated toxic pharmaceuticals and human sourced proteins within the scope of operating a portable sanitation business … In effect, we have established proprietary methods for the mining of human waste.' This 'human sourced protein production company' is also keen 'to obtain regulatory approval to market our thrombolytic agent, "Tru-Kinase" (our brand name for urokinase), throughout the world. Urokinase is presently approved and marketed worldwide. Our feedstock would be obtained from the urine supply in portable toilets owned by the host country cooperative venture. Our primary advantage is that we derive multiple products from a single source …'

But out of sight (and smell), out of mind – and a pill, wherever it comes from, is, of course, quicker, easier, more specific and more concentrated than the alternative. And safer – apart from the associated risks of picking up bacteria from unwashed or infected genitalia, the non-specific concentration of urine, and its sensitivity to bodily intake, mean that, while sodium might be beneficial to the undernourished, the salt-saturated Westerners recovering from heart attacks will be gulping down as much unneeded and detrimental salt in this tonic as they will the urokinase they're after. Similarly, if toxins seep into the body through environmental contamination of food, they will drain out again in concentrated form – not a leakage one really wants to reverse.

Even the Chinese Association of Urine Therapy admits that for novice imbibers (who might want to dilute their pee with fruit juice or water and honey until body, mind, and soul are accustomed to the taste), 'Common symptoms include diarrhoea, itch, pain, fatigue, soreness of the shoulder, fever, etc. These symptoms appear more frequently in patients suffering long term or more serious illnesses, and symptoms may repeat several times. Each episode may last 3–7 days, but sometimes it may last one month, or even worse over 6 months. It is a pity that many give up urine therapy because of such bad episode [sic]. Recovery reaction is just like the darkness before sunrise. If one persists and overcomes the difficulty, one can enjoy the eventual happiness of healthy life.'

Drinking urine is not a new idea; and however offputting these symptoms, for devotees of an eighteenth-century authority on drugs, piss might have seemed the lesser of available (beneficial) evils: in the 1759 edition of Lémery's

Dictionnaire universel des drogues simples, the author explains that 'All parts of man, his excrescences and excrements, contain oil and the sals volatile, combined with phlegm and earth ...', and proceeds to recommend not only the drinking of two or three glasses of urine each morning to cure gout, to relieve obstructions of the bowels and to dispel hysterical vapours, but also the burning of hair to counteract vapours; the saliva of a fasting young man to heal the bites of reptiles and mad dogs; well-chewed ear wax for the cure of whitlows (inflammation of a finger or toe near the nail); powdered toenail and fingernail shavings, washed down with wine, as a good emetic; a woman's milk for inflamed eyes; and human faeces, dried to combat epilepsy, or fresh for quinsy (suppurating tonsillitis) and anthrax.

Way back in the eleventh century, Chinese physicians reduced urine down to pearly white crystalline matter and then dissolved it in other drinks to conceal its 'unclean origins' from fastidious royal patrons – and they marketed it under the pure and pretty names of 'autumn mineral' and 'autumn ice'. Seventeenth- and eighteenth-century European doctors, among whom cow urine was a popular prescription for the vapours and gout, insomnia and epilepsy and vertigo, learnt the same lesson: the sick were treated with *l'eau de mille fleurs* and juices going by other such poetically harmless names. And we may smile and feel superior, but how many of us know or think of the major component of all the moisturizers and wrinkle-removers we smear on our skins today – it is urea.

Thus urine therapy has a long and illustrious history. Luminaries of the ancient world such as Hippocrates, the 'Father of Medicine', and the Roman physician Pliny, record the therapeutic use of urine (the latter preferring it to come from virginal boys). Thomas Lupton's *A thousand notable things of sundry sortes* (1579) also contains references to urine's curative properties. In the seventeenth century Robert Boyle, the 'father of chemistry', wrote that 'The medical virtues of man's urine, both inwardly given, and outwardly applied, would require rather a whole book, than a part of an essay, to enumerate and insist on', before briefly outlining the urinary happy ending of an 'ancient gentlewoman' plagued by 'divers chronic distempers'. Even today there is no shortage of volumes with titles like *The Golden Fountain* ..., *The Water of Life* ..., *Ein ganz besonderer Saft* ...[*A Very Special Juice* ...] and *Urine-Therapy: It May Save Your Life*.

Drinking is far from the only way of profiting from urine's plenty; indeed, not a limb or a crevice of the body seems unsusceptible to its restorative charms. AIDS sufferers have found it effective smeared on to viral infections of the skin; World War I soldiers might cure trench foot with piss (the water-sucking effect caused by the high osmotic pressure that urea creates helped to draw out infected and dead matter and to kill micro-organisms), or urinate into their boots before setting off on a march to help prevent blisters – the less organised might nurse blisters after the march by peeing on them (perhaps to draw out the serum) and then wrapping them in wool. Both soldiers and civilians would piss on their new leather boots or shoes to soften them (in the Second World War WAAFS and nurses stood their regulation shoes in the chamber pot to make them softer and less squeaky).

American boys used to urinate on their legs before swimming to prevent cramp, while schoolmasters used to use urine to harden their canes – hence the slang expression 'the rod's in piss' (or 'in pickle', i.e. 'preserved' for use) to mean that punishment loomed. Pee can apparently be gargled to fight gum or tongue disorders; or made into diluted eye drops for conjunctivitis or contact-lens tiredness; or dropped into the ears, and closed with cotton wool dipped in oil, for earaches and infections (reminiscent of the Italian pre-Renaissance trick of ousting parasitic worms from the ear canal with urine and wine); or sniffed from a bowl to unblock a stuffy nose or treat sinusitis; or poured into a foot- or hip-bath to improve circulation; or made into compresses for the anus and abdomen to cure haemorrhoids; or massaged into the skin for a lustrous sheen (follow up with aftershave if the smell disturbs), or the scalp for gleaming dandruff-free tresses; or applied as an enema – for who knows what purpose … In the deepest and most direct (and dangerous) application of all, a certain Florida doctor is said to inject his overweight patients with the urine of pregnant women to 'break down the fat cells' – though he puts them at the same time on a near-starvation diet, which may have more to do with his successes.

Piss has also been mixed, down the ages and across continents, with all manner of ingredients to alter the emphasis of its powers. The Aztecs washed wounds with a blend of urine, herbs and sweet aloe-like agave sap. Egyptian papyri speak of a burn salve of ground gourd seeds, salt and urine. Hindu practitioners of Ayurvedic medicine added herbs to make poultices, or herbs and curds to treat fevers, or milk to make 'soup', which was then evaporated off and its steam directed in pipes on to post-operative wounds. The Pericuis tribe of Lower California made a varnish of pee and coal to coat their children's faces as armour against the weather. Affectionate American mothers were reported in the early nineteenth century to treat their kids to a 'buttered flip', made of fresh urine, hot water, honey and a knob of butter – a variation on the more adult version of hot sweetened beer and spirits.

And human urine is not alone. Following in the Ayurvedic medicinal tradition, with its five key ingredients of butter, milk, curd, dung and urine, collectively known as panchgavya, cow's piss is being newly touted as a cure-all in India. It is supplied by a cooperative in the northern 'cow-belt' state of Uttar Pradesh – thus promoting village industry – and is flying off the shelves of goratna (cow-products) stalls in New Delhi, in the form of potions and pills to cure cancer and constipation, diabetes and 'ladies' diseases'; in particular, a delighted vendor boasts, 'the constipation medicine is a hot seller.' A spokesman for the Hindu nationalist BJP, which has long campaigned for the sanctity of the cow, warns that shampoo may be next.

Chinese Eggs ...

Reports from eastern China tell of queues of boys, piss-filled washbasin in hand, besieging every primary school for the modest remuneration offered for a slug of fresh boy's pee. Its destination: the saucepans of egg-boiling citizens keen to get longer life along with their protein. In a much-mutated version of the ancient Ayurvedic traditions, and of Chinese emperors' retinues of young boys, kept at the behest of the court physicians solely to produce their inimitable nectar, some modern Chinese are clutching at pseudo-scientific straws in the search for youthful health. Children's urine is indeed rich in excreted human growth hormone (HGH) – and the preference for boys' reflects both the ubiquitous Asian favouring of the male and the greater physical ease of collection from their inbuilt 'delivery spigot' – not to mention their probably greater readiness to drop their trousers and earn some quick cash. The semi-permeable membrane of an eggshell would indeed allow some of the contents of the urine to pass into the egg; and defendants claim that the homeopathic 'priming' of bodily systems through small doses of a natural substance can stimulate a beneficial autologous response – but the likelihood is small of getting more from your pee-infused egg than the useless remnants of a hormone broken up by digestion, and a slightly odd breakfast-time flavour.

... and Indian Olives

The culinary speciality of the Chinook Indians was less a remedy than a delicacy, described by one American traveller as 'Chinook olives' – acorns soaked for five months in human urine.

Five

Quirky Recreations

The Urinal Game

Several versions of this game vie on the Web for status as the most addictive, not to mention educational, activity involving a urinal. A personal favourite explains the task thus: 'The object of the game is to test your knowledge of men's room etiquette. You will be presented with several scenarios. In each one you must select the proper urinal to use. Click on the door to enter.' I enter and am greeted by the sight of six urinals in a row, with a door at one end and the urinal furthest from the door half-hidden by a round-backed little man: 'Urinal One is occupied. Select the correct urinal for you to use. Click on your choice.' I choose six, next to the door, and to my delight, 'Urinal Six is the correct answer. Going to Urinal Six gives you the maximum amount of buffer zone. It also shows proper respect of the personal space of your bathroom buddy. Click on the door to continue.' I do; I can't resist; I work my way through a series of variously inhabited men's rooms, and am reprimanded for my occasional errors with phrases which patiently explain that my choice 'gives the appearance that you and he might be pairing up', or 'would put you between other people. That is just too much pressure for a man to take,' or, when all the odd numbers are already taken, the consolatory advice that 'This is really an awkward situation. To avoid the appearance of pairing you should normally avoid being next to someone else. However, in this case, you are close to the door and able to make a quick exit. Don't worry about washing your hands. Just get out as fast as you can.' When I take up a dangerous position beside a wide-shouldered skinhead I am asked, suspiciously, 'Is there some reason you want to be alone with the big lug? … you should never leave any question as to your manliness.' Finally, the pièce de résistance, the insoluble quandary: numbers two, four and six are taken; I choose five – but 'The only real solution to this puzzle was to turn around and walk out of the door, wait a little while, then come back in.' Then the politest of postscripts: 'Thank you for trying our little test. We hope you found it educational and helpful. Before you go be sure to wash your hands. Click on the door to play again.' And I do.

You're in Control (Urine Control)

Taking play with piss to the height of seriousness, two MIT students, Hayes Solos Raffle and Dan Maynes-Aminzade, brought to fruition a desire to 'question how technology can both challenge and enforce social mores' in their 2002 final project. 'On one hand, *You're In Control* questions a basic social code of privacy by assuming that public urination is acceptable if the participant is playing a computer game. On the other hand, *You're In Control* proposes the application of technology to positively enforce social codes of sanitation.' So what is it? It is a video game in a urinal, in which the link between gamer and screen is the stream of piss.

In-depth documentation tells how, having been donated a urinal destined for the landfill, the students overcome the complex problems of pressure-sensing (with such remedies as 'custom-tuning the following amplifying circuits to deliver clear signals to the microprocessor'); analyse analogue inputs and decide they need digital; mount their electronics on a large breadboard, in turn mounted behind the urinal ('The complete circuit includes 16 1.5" piezoceramic buzzers (our sensors), 16 amplifying circuits, a 16F877 PIC chip, a serial line driver for the PIC to talk to a PC, and a 5V power regulator to keep everything running smoothly'), which is itself mounted on 'a sheetrock wall to create a convincing interactive experience'; run the sensor wires through the shiny chrome-plated plumbing fixtures (this urinal has no flush); and finally mount a video/audio screen on the back of the wall with gaffer tape.'The white wall and placard made reference to art installations, where the urinal has a rich history. The video game is our interpretation of the classic carnival game "whack-a-mole."'

'Position on the back of the urinal corresponds to position on the screen. The player attempted to hit hamsters as they jumped from one hole in the ground into another hole in the ground. A successful hit turned the hamster yellow, made it scream and spin out of control, and rewarded the player with ten points. The parabolic paths of the hamsters concealed the grid-like arrangement of sensors, resulting in a fluid transition between input and output. The game was programmed in C++ on the Windows 2000 operating system.' And so as not to deprive the girls of their gaming thrills, there's a 'customized game controller', an irreverent hybrid of 'Nintendo-style game controllers, plumbing equipment, and strap-on dildo harnesses. The oversized phallic nozzle is powered by two water reservoirs located to suggest oversized ovaries, making it oddly hermaphroditic. The controller consists of a nylon belt, a formed acrylic pelvic plate, water bottles, tubing, and a flexible garden hose nozzle. It is worn around the waist and the bottles are gripped and squeezed to pressurize a stream of water.' And to the pair's delight, it all works first time, and their guinea pigs are quick and keen learners, and they nurse their ambitions of bringing their cute prototype into the big bad world of the real restroom. 'We hope that further developments of *You're In Control* will help encourage restroom cleanliness while reintroducing play to the act of peeing.'

Watersports

Urophilia (*uro* denoting urine, from the Greek *ouron*, and *philein*, to love) and urolagnia (*lagneia*, lust) are words denoting the sexual arousal caused by, or associated with, urine or urination. This stimulation might take the form of peeing in public, peeing on others or being peed on, drinking the pee, or watching others do any of this – not to be confused with the sadomasochistic tendency that makes someone with an uncomfortably or painfully full bladder seem highly sexually attractive. Because healthy urine is sterile, such sexual practices are usually quite safe; otherwise, unromantic results might include the transmission of disease, or of any bacterial infection present in the urethra; or secondary effects like skin rashes. In *Studies in the Psychology of Sex*, Havelock Ellis, who preceded Freud in the study of sexual behaviour, recounts many cases of people obtaining sexual excitement by seeing others urinating, and also by drinking the urine. In one case, he says, a young man 'found complete satisfaction in drinking the still hot urine of women. When a lady or girl in the house went to her room to satisfy a need of this kind [in a chamber pot], she had hardly left it but he hastened in, overcome by extreme excitement, culminating in spontaneous ejaculation. The younger the woman, the greater the transport he experienced.' According to Roy Eskapa, Havelock Ellis himself was supposed to be aroused by seeing women weeing, ever since having seen his mother squat and pee on a side-path at London Zoo.

Finally, for the young and the young at heart, there's a whole host of songs and sayings easy to lavatorialize; nursery rhymes are just the beginning ...

Hey diddle diddle, the cat did a widdle
The cow did a plop on the moon.

Six

Religion, Superstition and Spirituality

When he urinated, it sounded like night prayer. (F. Scott Fitzgerald, *Notebooks*, M)

Christianity

Urinophiles delight in reading every one of the Bible's references to water as references to urine. Among the favourites are 'The law of the wise is a fountain of life, to depart from the snares of death' (Proverbs 13:14 – all references are to the Authorised Version unless otherwise stated); 'the water that I shall give him shall be a well of water springing up into everlasting life' (John 4:14); and 'He that believeth on me, as the scripture hath said, out of his belly shall flow rivers of living water' (John 7:38) – though the only one that seems remotely convincing is the ubiquitous 'Drink waters out of thine own cistern, and running waters out of thine own well' (Proverbs 5:15).

But the only biblical forms in which piss explicitly springs forth are less elevated: God vows to 'cut off from Jeroboam him that pisseth against the wall' (1 Kings 14:10), and curses the house of Ahab in the same way in 21:21, and again in 2 Kings 9:8; David previously has pledged the same, in 1 Samuel 25:22,34; then, in Kings 16:11–12, Zimri actually does it, to the whole of the house of Baasha, 'according to the word of the Lord' (and comes to a sticky end for his treasonous deeds). The meaning of 'him that pisseth against the wall' is apparently simply 'male person,' since the New English Bible has here 'every mother's son ...', the New International Version 'every last male.'

Judaism

Jewish urine is subject to typically fantastical contortions of reading and rereading. The halakhot – Jewish ritual and civil laws, as opposed to theological or devotional matters – include the following:

> It is forbidden to read K'riat Sh'ma while facing human tzo'ah [faeces], or tzo'ah of dogs or pigs while they have hides in them or any tzo'ah which has a foul smell like these. Similarly, [it is forbidden to read] facing human urine. However, it is permissible [to read] while facing animal urine.
>
> Urine that was absorbed in the ground – if it could still wet the hand [that touches it], it is forbidden to read facing it; if not, it is permissible.
>
> How far does a person have to distance himself from tzo'ah or urine and then to read? 4 Amot [a measure of

length, lit. 'forearm' – approx. 18–24 inches], when it was behind or beside him; however, if it was facing him, he must distance himself until he can no longer see it, and then read.

This applied when it was in the same room, on the same level; however, if there was a place there higher or lower than it by 10 Tefahim [a hand's breadth – between 3 and 4 inches], he may sit right next to that place and read, since there is a barrier there – as long as the foul smell doesn't reach him. Similarly, if he covered the tzo'ah or urine with a vessel, even if they are in the same room as he is, it is as if it is buried and it is permissible to read facing it. (Kriat Shema 3:6–9)

According to the Gemara, you must stop saying the Shemoneh Esreh (a prayer at the centre of the three daily services) if urine is dripping from you, and wait until the flow ceases, but you are allowed to resume the reading when there is urine on your body and clothing – even though the Mishnah (an early written compilation of Jewish oral tradition) states that one may not pray near urine. One answer to the contradiction is that if the urine is absorbed by something, and not wet enough to make something else wet, then it's all right; another draws the distinction between the prohibitions from the Torah – set in stone – and those from the rabbis – less weighty: the former says that you mustn't pray in front of the *flow* of urine as it leaves the body; when it is no longer flowing, but resting in front of the praying or on their clothes, the prohibition is only of the rabbinic sort – and even this wasn't enforced if prayer had already begun; rabbis only prohibited *beginning* to pray in front of urine. And so the complications multiply.

Islam

Some words of advice from one of Islam's most famous spokesman, Ayatollah Khomeini:

> If one commits the act of sodomy with a cow, an ewe, or a camel, their urine and their excrements become impure, and even their milk may no longer be consumed. The animal must then be killed and as quickly as possible and burned. (From *The Little Green Book: Sayings of Ayatollah Khomeini, Political, Phylosophica, Social and Religious*, 47, source: Homa)

> Eleven things are impure: urine, excrement, sperm ... non-Moslem men and women ... and the sweat of an excrement-eating camel. (From *The Little Green Book*, source: Harwood's *Mythology's Last Gods*, 175)

The Hadith – stories about the sayings and doings of the Prophet – contain lots of home remedies – such as drinking camel urine to recuperate after illness (Hadith 590, p.399, vol.7). But spilling the secret of this medicine did the Prophet – and in the end his healed enemies – no favours:

> Anas said, "Some people of 'Ukl or 'Uraina tribe came to Medina and its climate did not suit them. So the Prophet ordered them to go to the herd of (Milch) camels and to drink their milk and urine (as a medicine). So they went as directed and after they became healthy, they killed the

shepherd of the Prophet and drove away all the camels. The news reached the Prophet early in the morning and he sent (men) in their pursuit and they were captured and brought at noon. He then ordered to cut their hands and feet (and it was done), and their eyes were branded with heated pieces of iron. They were put in 'Al-Harra' and when they asked for water, no water was given to them." Abu Qilaba said, "Those people committed theft and murder, became infidels after embracing Islam and fought against Allah and His Apostle" (vol.1, book 4, number 234; narrated Abu Qilaba).

More obliquely, Al Hadis, Book 1, Chap 8, No. 58 – Abdullah-b-Sarjas reports that the Messenger of Allah said: 'None of you must pass urine in a snake's hole' (Attested by Nisai, Abu Daud).

Buddhism

Buddha teaches a lesson which is well known to all reluctant young green-bean-eaters, that what's good for you might not always taste divine: "Bhikkhus, a man would come along suffering from jaundice and he is told: Friend, there is a drink made out of putrid urine, with various kinds of medicines put in it. If you desire drink. When drinking it would not be agreeable to sight, smell or taste but drinking it you will get over your illness. He reflects about it and drinks it. It would not be agreeable to sight, smell or taste, yet he would get over that illness. I say this observance of the Teaching is comparable to this, as it is now unpleasant and brings pleasant results in the future" (the Buddha's words from MN46 'Maha-dhamma-samadana Sutta', The Longer Discourse on Observation).

The ascetic Buddhist monk, the bhikkhu, relies for his mecidinal needs on puti-mutta-bhesajja – a substance which translates literally as 'rancid urine medicine'. In Sri Lanka, the magic formula is usually medicinal fruits pickled in cow's urine; in Thailand, some use their own first urine of the day, in the ancient Indian tradition of such a tonic.

Folk Magic

Urine is a valuable ingredient in many hoodoo, rootwork and folk-magical spells, coming, on a par with faeces, sweat, blood and spit, second only to the genital fluids in its potency as a 'magical link' – for which inferior substitutes include (in descending order of strength) the hair, unwashed clothing, nail clippings, handwriting and a photograph of the target. A woman can use it instead of menstrual blood, pouring it into a cup of coffee that will make a man hers for ever; she can urinate on a gambler's mojo hand (the central amulet in African-American hoodoo, a bag made of flannel and filled with magic objects) to bring him luck. A floor wash of warm water, salt, saltpetre and one's own first urine of the day, scrubbed in silence from the doorway out towards the pavement, will ward off all evil. But while one's own urine can be a source of strength and fortune, in enemy hands it is one's vulnerability: piss in a bottle with red pepper and the soil of a graveyard can bring on urinary tract problems from cystitis to kidney stones – ending only when the bottle is smashed and the urine drained away into a fire. Urine is a weapon of seduction and attack and of counter-attack: a man cursed with impotence can cure it by pissing into a red-ants' nest.

Many more spells feature women's urine than men's (and most spells featuring urine are linked to love or lust), and their effectiveness is sometimes explained as an amplification of the natural way in which a female attracts a male – so that while its magical deployment has been compared to animal scent marking, used by males to drive off rivals, it is more comparable to animal communication of the female sexual state, by the sniffing or even the tasting of her urine by the male. And while female humans are attracted to male under-arm scents (rich in the pheromone androsterone), male humans are attracted to female vaginal scents, which include lingering urinal odours known as copulins, pheromones whose composition changes throughout the monthly cycle; if these function as territorial markers, it is only to other females. Hence men are at the mercy of women's pee, and are taught to avoid cooking that can easily camouflage it – not only coffee, but spaghetti bolognaise, might have been adulterated in the kitchen by a ruthless bella donna or her matriarchal mama.

Soma

There is an old shamanistic tradition of eating the *amanita muscaria* mushroom and recycling its effects by urinating and giving the liquid to others to drink – including reindeer (see pages 179–182). This may have spread from Siberia to pre-Brahman India, and inspired the Vedic Soma. The Veda are the four most ancient texts of the Hindu religion (estimates of their date range from 2,500 to 1,500 BC), and much space in them is devoted to the ritual consumption of a psychoactive drug called *soma* (Sanskrit for 'pressed juice'). Despite all the hymns of prolix praise, this *soma* is only ever alluded to obliquely, by means of copious word-play and elaborate poetic tropes – and has unleashed a millennia-long identity-hunt amongst the pious and the curious. It is clear that *soma* is a plant, and induces mental ecstasy – but thousands of psychoactive plants could fit the bill. Further clues suggest that it is leafless and branchless, with a heavy stalk, and picked on mountain sides, by moonlight, then reduced to a liquid of golden yellow, or morning yellow, or the colour of fire, of fire in the morning … and eaten with either milk or butter or both.

In 1968, R. Gordon Wasson's *SOMA: The Divine Mushroom of Immortality* proposed a set of reasons for which the *soma* must be the *amanita muscaria*, the divine mushroom of the title. He pointed out that *soma* is mentioned in *The Rig Veda* in connection with urine: 'Acting in concert, those charged with the office, richly gifted, do full homage to Soma. The swollen men piss the flowing [*soma*]'. Drinking in turn provides the link to the fly-agaric mushroom, the only plant-derived intoxicant which is not only incompletely metabolized by the liver and can therefore be recycled by urine-drinking, but also has a known tradition of urine-drinking associated with it (see pages 179–182).

The Buddhist *Legend About Chakdor* tells the story of the origin of *amrita*, and provides the crucial link between *soma* and urine-drinking; to this day, the drinking of a potion called *amrita* is central to Vajrayana Buddhist rituals. This is now generally just coloured water, but is imaginatively invested with psychoactive properties in the context of an initiation – which suggests that the modern liquid is a symbolic, literally watered-down version of an original potent potion. It seems clear that urine was the elixir, the golden-yellow liquid that let the drinker be at once in the physical world and in the spiritual – leading, perhaps, to the sanctity, in Indo-Iranian tradition, of urine itself, beyond any chance fungal companions to its powers.

In a variation on the Siberian cooperation with the reindeer, *soma* was also given to a bull, and its urine drunk – as today both urine and faeces of a cow are partaken of in some purificatory ceremonies.

The Twenty-first Century

Nor does urine lack its latter-day worshippers, often within a blend of more conventional religions: one 'Naturopathic Urine Therapist's' website proclaims 'Jesus' Diet for Your Sins' and quotes not only biblical inspirations – 'If you believe in me, you will never thirst' (John 6:35); 'Rivers of living water shall flow from your bellies' (John 7:38) – but encouragements ranging from the pseudo-scientific – 'Urine is a medicinal, cleansing, and nourishing food ... with a surprising ability to cure an amazing variety of ills ... which has been scientifically-proven, and medically-documented'

– to the unashamedly spiritually woolly: 'The life ("life-force") of the flesh is in the blood, and as urine comes from the blood, it contains that life-force ...'

One of the preacher's holy texts is Coen van der Kroon's *The Golden Fountain: The Complete Guide to Urine Therapy*, which, in addition to piquant illustrations of Indian holy men sipping piss from human skulls, gives a translation of the 107 verses of the ancient Sanskrit text *Shivambu Kalpa Vidhi* ('the method of drinking urine for rejuvenation').

Urine-drinking combined with dietary restrictions and periods of fasting, in a practice known as *amoroli*, may have been effective in promoting the meditative state – not least from what we know now to be the melatonin, a hormone of tranquillizing effect, present in urine. Allegedly, the 'divine nectar ... is capable of abolishing old age ... All the ailments subject to from the very birth will be completely cured ... One's body will be internally cleansed ... Drinking it for two months stimulates and energizes the senses ... Followed for three months, all types of ailments will disappear and all miseries will evaporate ... After five months, the follower will be completely healthy, and will be bestowed with divine eyesight ... After six months, the follower will be exceptionally intelligent ... After seven months, the follower will be exceptionally strong ... After eight months, the human body will possess divine lustre, like that of shining gold, that will be permanent ... After nine months of continual use, tuberculosis and leprosy will perish ... After ten months of continual use, the follower becomes practically the treasury of lustre and brightness ... After eleven months, the follower becomes pure, both externally and internally ... After one year of continual use, the follower acquires solar shining ...

'Seven years of use makes the follower capable of conquering his ego ... Nine years of this method will make the follower immortal ... After ten years of experimentation, it will be possible to float in the air with ease ... Twelve years will enable one to be as long lived as the moon and the planets ... Dangerous animals such as serpents will not affect one in any way; serpents' poison will not kill the follower. One can float on water just as wood floats, and he will never drown ... (verses 9-21).'

Seven

Testing

For Illness

If thou couldst, doctor, cast
The water of my land, find her disease,
And purge it to a sound and pristine health,
I would applaud thee to the very echo,
That should applaud again.

Macbeth, V. iii

U rine was commonly used in the ancient world for treating ailments (see pages 32–3), and also in their diagnosis. The term 'diabetes mellitus', for example, originates in pre-Christian Greece: 'diabetes' comes from the verb 'diabainein', meaning 'to pass through'; hence its derivative 'diabētēs' means a siphon, or specifically one who discharges excessive amounts of urine. 'Mellitus', meanwhile, is from the same root as 'meli', honey. So Greek physicians must have known not only that diabetics pee a lot, but that their pee is full of sugar; and since they lacked the chemical knowledge and analytical techniques to have found this out any other way, they must have simply tasted it. Indeed, medical texts from the Ancient Greeks to the present advise on what can be learnt of the patient by how their pee looks, smells and tastes; modern techniques and instruments just improve upon what the eyes, nose and mouth have done for millennia.

When these practices were first graced with a name, it was uroscopy, and was carried out by doctors commonly known as piss-prophets (a term attested from 1625). Urine would be collected for medical examination in a glass bottle called a jordan (also a more general term for chamber pot – perhaps short for Jordan-bottle, originally a bottle of water brought from the River Jordan by crusaders or pilgrims). In the middle of the seventeenth century jordans were often called 'looking glasses' – though the doctor hoped to see not his own reflection but the patient's: as John Collop wrote,

Hence looking-glasses, chamber pots we call,
'Cause in your pisse we can discover all.

Piss-prophesying was a dangerous business in those early days. In 1382 Roger Clerk of Wandsworth, convicted of pretending to have medical and prophetic knowledge, was sentenced to ride through London, facing the horse's tail, with two jordans hung round his neck. A little pretence might be excusable in some cases, though, if not always effective. Sir Thomas More, imprisoned in the Tower of London for refusing to support Henry VIII in his marital antics, received a message from the King to ask whether he had changed his mind. He said yes, he had, and so a councillor was sent to get his formal agreement. 'Oh no!'

he said; 'I have not changed my mind about that; but I had planned to send for a barber, to be shaved before I died, but now if it please the King, he shall cut off my head and my beard, and all together!' Then he called for his urinal, and (according to Sir John Harington), 'having made water in it, he cast it, and viewed it (as Physicians do) a pretie while; at last he sware soberly, that he saw nothing in that man's water, but that he might live, if it pleased the King.' But the King was unmoved, and More was beheaded.

The modern, less colourful, incarnation of these techniques is urinalysis, the examination of urine by a variety of chemical and microscopic tests to look for infections of the urinary tract, kidney disease, and related problems.

To collect a 'clean-catch' (midstream) urine sample, simply wipe the genital area, release a little pee to clear the urethra of contaminants, then catch a slug of liquid in a clean container and remove the container from the urine stream. Just as for the pee-drinkers, the first urine of the day is best, since it is most concentrated and so most likely to reveal abnormalities. Tests generally use sticks like cotton buds; the pads are impregnated with chemicals that change colour to indicate the materials of interest.

Chemical examination can test for, amongst other things: urine appearance and colour; haemoglobin (which carries oxygen in red blood cells) or a product of its degradation, bilirubin; glucose; and urine ketones (by-products of fat metabolism, present in the starving and the diabetic). It can also measure the urine's pH (its acidity or alkalinity) and its specific gravity. A microscopic examination can reveal bacteria and other micro-organisms, crystals, fat, mucus, red blood cells (signalling damaged tubules), nitrites and white blood cells (indicators of urinary tract infection), and various other cells and indigestible matter.

The colour of normal urine can vary from almost colourless to dark yellow (and things as harmless as beetroots and blackberries can act as drastic dyes). The density of the urine varies slightly according to the time of day and the behaviour of the subject; kidney disease can produce a change.

The normal pH range is from 4.6 (acid) to 8.0 (alkaline), with an average of 6.0, and is also influenced by a number of factors. Alkaline urine makes formation of kidney stones less likely, and favours the action of antibiotics, but acidic urine stops other sorts of stones and bacteria from growing.

There should be no detectable haemoglobin or bilirubin (which means liver or bile duct disease), or glucose, ketones, protein (one of the best indicators of kidney disease), nor red blood cells (which might be the result of urinary tract disease or bleeding from the kidneys, though equally of vigorous physical exercise) or white blood cells (along with nitrites, signs of a urinary tract infection). If the subject has been trying to ward off a cold with citrus fruits and vitamin pills, excess excreted vitamin C (like many other more complex drugs) can interfere with the tests, giving both false positives and false negatives. But in general, the tests can be reliably performed under conditions of – and illuminate the extent or nature of – a myriad of conditions from anorexia to dementia, heart failure to ovarian cancer, bladder stones to incontinence.

In diabetes, urine can be of help in both diagnosis and ongoing monitoring: the warning signs might include constant thirst and more frequent urination, and regular testing for ketones and protein in the urine keeps tabs on the ups and downs of the disease, which is characterized by varying or persistent hyperglycaemia (elevated blood-sugar levels) after eating. This failure to use sugar and starch properly is caused in diabetes mellitus type 1 by decreased production of the regulating hormone insulin by the pancreas, in type 2 (usually late-onset) by decreased sensitivity to it. As a result, glucose accumulates in the blood and tissues, and the sufferer has to try to keep blood sugar within normal limits, so as so lessen the risk of complications such as heart and liver disease, blindness and nerve damage.

Insulin is needed for cells to use sugar for energy. If they can't get enough insulin they stop using sugar and turn to fat instead; and when fat is broken down, ketones are made. Ketones may make the urine smell sweet (think nail-varnish remover) but they are harmful to the body; ketones in the urine may be a sign of diabetic ketoacidosis, the stage that follows hyperglycaemia.

Diabetes isn't just a human problem; cats and dogs get it too, and their owners face many problems in collecting and testing their urine and injecting them with insulin.

Artificial urine can also be manufactured for use by medical students, to allow them to practise clinical testing in the laboratory without running the risk of accidental contamination with potentially fatal pathogens. It can be bought or made up locally, and dosed with particular ingredients to simulate diseases.

For Pregnancy

Just as do-it-yourself kits for illness-testing are available, allowing hypochondriacs to minimize their life expectancies by imaginative reading of the colour chart, so those with morning-after anxieties can now silence or confirm them with home pregnancy testing, which checks for the presence of the hormone hCG (human chorionic gonadotropin) – produced by the placenta and detectable in the urine (and the blood) as early as ten days after fertilization – by the use of specialized antibodies which clot with the hCG molecules: if this reaction occurs, the test is positive, and, in over-the-counter versions, will make the test strip change colour in a matter of minutes. False results may occur when there is blood or protein in the urine, or a urinary tract infection; if the test is carried out too early (the amounts of hormone increase throughout the first three months); if the urine is not concentrated enough (the first urine of the day is best); or if the pregnancy itself is somehow abnormal.

Laboratory blood tests can confirm pregnancy just a week after conception; and can also be used after the basic qualitative blood or urine test to provide more detailed, quantitative information about the hormone levels. The home-use kits come in countless guises, from those with a round window in which a line appears, to those with digital readouts declaring you 'Pregnant' or 'Not Pregnant'; some for mid-stream use, others with a pipette for a collected sample; and all mail-order versions promising discreetly unmarked packaging …

Rather less elaborate is the earliest-known pregnancy test, described, on a papyrus of ancient Egyptian medical practices and rites, as the 'Barley and Emmer' test (emmer is a kind of wheat): 'The woman must moisten it with urine every day … if both grow, she will give birth. If the barley grows, it means a male child. If the emmer grows, it means a female child. If neither grows she will not give birth.' Primitive and implausible it may seem – but modern experiments have shown that the urine of a woman who is not pregnant will prevent the growth of barley – so that the sexual distinction between wheat and barley may have been a little over-ambitious, but answers to the essential baby/no baby question might well have been far from nonsensical.

A little closer to today's incarnation is the rabbit test: in the 1920s, researchers discovered that hCG was present in the urine of pregnant women, and that if a female rabbit was injected with this piss, the rabbit's ovaries would display distinct changes within days. A common misconception is that if the woman was pregnant the rabbit died. In fact the rabbit had to be killed anyway for its ovaries to be examined (in an episode of TV's long-running black comedy M*A*S*H* entitled 'What's Up, Doc?', there is a tentative explanation of the principles to a loving rabbit-owner, and his slowly dawning comprehension:'… You're not gonna use my rabbit as a guinea-pig! That would be murder!'). But the phrase 'the rabbit died' lives on as a euphemism for a positive pregnancy test, as does the principle of hCG detection in the urine – although without the rabbit.

For Drugs

Ever more ubiquitous is drug testing, assessing suspects from athletes to schoolkids for their recent intake, performance-enhancing or recreational. As with pregnancy tests, there are two potential stages in the drug testing process: the immunoassay test and the gas chromatography/mass spectrometry (GC/MS) test. The former can be performed instantly and on-site, but has an approximate five per cent false-positive error rate, meaning urine that tested positive used to have to be sent to a certified laboratory for confirmation by the 100-per-cent-accurate drugs-testing 'gold standard'. Now, however, the two come in one, including a version suitable for home use.

While Ancient Greek Olympians and gladiators improved their performance with potions and proteins, their modern descendants have made the Olympics an ever bloodier battlefield in the war on drugs in sport. At the 2004 Athens Games, for the first time in Olympic history, all competitors were subject to blood testing as well as the conventional urine testing for drugs. Over 500 doping-control staff oversaw some 3,500 blood and urine tests, observed by hawk-eyed independent witnesses from the World Anti-Doping Agency. The authorities progress in step with the cheats – though it's never quite clear who is that crucial half-step ahead.

At the Sydney 2000 games testing for EPO (erythropoietin, which improves the oxygen-carrying capacity of the blood) was introduced, by means of both a urine and a blood test; as of Athens 2004 detection could be done with urine alone. The other main focuses in Athens were the 'designer' (i.e. designed specifically to avoid detection) steroid THG (tetrahydroges-trinone, tested with urine, and at the centre of a doping scandal which tore apart American athletics), and hGH (human growth hormone – known as 'the sprinter's Viagra', which works like an anabolic steroid, to build muscle and aid recovery from training, and is thought to be one of the most widely used banned substances in sports; until now, controls have been unable to distinguish between the naturally-produced hormone and the synthetic version). The test for hGH was being developed against the clock up till the last minute – and in the end was ready, but effective only using blood.

There were random blood and urine tests for athletes two weeks before and during the qualifying heats; then a random test of one athlete in each event; followed by tests of all the medal-winners. The athlete's name would be allocated to a doping-control escort, who had then to scour the village in search of them, notify them and keep them under close observation until they reported for testing. The athlete could choose to be accompanied by a representative, who could be present for the blood test but not the urine – this would be witnessed by a chaperone of the same sex as the athlete. If there was not enough urine for a sample – the athlete was allowed to have a drink of water beforehand – or it was of unsuitable acidity or concentration, they could be asked to pee again. Half of each of the two (anonymous) samples would then be sent off for analysis. The laboratory could process 180 a day, churning out negative results within 24 hours and positive in 36. In the case of positive results, a disciplinary commission would be set up and inform the athletes, who would have the right to see the unused half of their sample opened and analysed in front of them, and later to defend themselves at the disciplinary hearing. As a result of all this, a handful of disgraced winners were stripped of their medals; and the gold-medal-winning Hungarian hammer-thrower, Adrian Annus, was chased across Europe on suspicion of having switched urine tests after his victory – his friend and compatriot, Robert Fazekas, was stripped of the discus gold, though his defence claimed this was as a result of a rare medical condition, paruesis, which makes it impossible to 'go' at will.

One champion 100-metre sprinter told the BBC that cheating in sports is as much a part of human nature as cheating in taxes, tests and relationships; that we cheat till we get caught – because we think we never could be; and that the problems of cheating are less than the problems of going straight.

More controversial than trying to keep competitors on an equal footing is the attempt to keep tabs on recreational drug use. In the United States a Supreme Court ruling was passed on a case in Oklahoma in 2002, supporting the initiation of a Student Activities Drug Testing Policy by a School District authority. This requires pupils to consent to drug testing in order to join in after-school clubs 'such as the Academic Team, Future Farmers of America, Future Homemakers of America, band, choir, pom-pom, cheerleading, and athletics.' The urinalysis tests are designed to detect the use of illegal drugs including amphetamines, marijuana, cocaine, opiates and barbiturates – not medical conditions or prescribed medications. A monitor waits outside the toilet cubicle for the pupil to produce a sample, and must 'listen for the normal sounds of urination in order to guard against tampered specimens and to insure an accurate chain of custody', before pouring the urine into two bottles, sealing them, and sending them off, together with a consent form signed by the pupil.

Results are kept separate from other educational records, released only on a 'need-to-know' basis; nor is there any connection with the police. One failed test means a parental notification. After drug counselling and a second, clear, test, admission to the club is allowed; but a second positive leads to suspension from all clubs, four compulsory hours of 'substance abuse counselling' and monthly tests thereafter; three positives means you're out of the extracurricular programme for the year.

The hearing went through stage after stage of challenge, appeal, reversal and upholding: the Fourth Amendment was cited, which protects the 'right of the people to be secure in their persons, houses, papers, and effects, against unreasonable searches and seizures'. The concepts of 'legitimate concern', 'proven problem' ('marijuana cigarettes near the school parking lot', 'drugs or drug paraphernalia in a car driven by a Future Farmers of America member'), 'prevention of the development of hazardous conditions', 'reasonableness', 'benefit to students or school' and 'surpassing safety interests' were all invoked. While schoolchildren do not shed their constitutional rights when they enter the schoolhouse, it seems their rights are different there from elsewhere – 'reasonableness' is countered by 'custodial and tutelary responsibility', doing away with the need for 'individualized suspicion' in 'a fact-specific balancing of the intrusion on the children's Fourth Amendment rights against the promotion of legitimate governmental interests.'

Urine becomes the pungent symbol of a veritable torrent of legality and morality.

Opponents of the new measures say that since cannabis remains detectable in the urine for up to a month, where alcohol, heroin and cocaine fade from it in a day or two, testing will only encourage kids to switch to more dangerous drugs; they argue that keeping kids active and learning after school is the best way of keeping them off drugs – and that those most likely to participate are anyway those least likely to be using, while those who are found to be using will be banned and left thereafter to their own devices.

They also suggest that those more sensitive souls who prefer on principle to keep their bodily fluids to themselves, or consider urine testing a gross invasion of privacy, will, absurdly, be kept away from the choir and the cookery club altogether; that extra-curricular activities build a sense of citizenship and leadership, while being told to urinate into a cup within earshot of an intently listening member of school authority, and then to turn the urine over for chemical examination, can do nothing but harm to society beyond the school gates; that kids should see their teachers as mentors who can offer anonymous help rather than as an extension of the police force; and that the programmes cost millions and achieve nothing.

The very day after the ruling, Psychemedics, a company that markets hair tests for MDMA and other illegal drugs, pronounced the decision to be very good for business. Others fill their literature with capitalized hyperbole – 'From Harmless Fun to Family Breakdown' – and sell their urinary espionage services ('For the price of the test you get free confirmation lab testing of preliminary positive results, referrals to professional family counselors and free educational materials – including family contracts') as 'A Tool to Help Build Trust'. The critics consider the ruling a topsy-turvy one: Glen Boire, of the Center for Cognitive Liberty and Ethics, angrily and evocatively conveys the absurd legality that gives 'the insides of students' bodies less protection than the insides of their backpacks, the contents of their bodily fluids less protection than the contents of their telephone calls […] what society presently regards as a "reasonable expectation of privacy" will be considerably watered down'; 'rivers of urine' will erode constitutional rights, raising the 'myopic hysteria' of the 'zero-tolerance' War on Drugs above the respect for and dignity of the nation's young people, who become permanent suspects required to prove their innocence rather than innocents whose guilt has to be proven. Each bottle of urine is one more marker of the fragility of the freedoms of the individual and the failure of the War on Drugs.

Then there's workplace testing, used most commonly to check out applicants, but also after accidents to determine their cause, as part of a routine physical check-up, randomly

– usually in jobs involving security or public safety – and as follow-up to treatment, to monitor an employee's success in staying clean.

The Anti-test

As the urine police proliferate, so do those who feed off their targets' fear, peddling detox products and self-test kits to check their efficacy. A Randomizer Urine Additive, for example, promises to eliminate all toxins in a urine sample in five seconds, even THC metabolites (from the main intoxicant substance in cannabis); promises easier mixing, as a liquid, than competitors' crystals – 'No Waiting, No Mixing. No Nitrates and No Nitrites'. Then there are the anti-anti-tests: the Drug Adulteration Strips that determine whether urine has been adulterated in order to pass or block a drugs test. These check for nitrites, oxidants and glutaraldehyde, which are ingredients of many drug-test blocking products; creatinine and specific gravity levels, to ascertain whether the urine has been watered down; and pH level, to see whether chlorine bleach has been added to the urine.

Nonetheless, the detection-dodgers are hard to quash. Certain companies (peopled by ex-drug-testing-facility managers, absconders from vitamin and mineral manufacturers, or nutritional-science experts) give multiple tailor-made options for detox suited to every occasion – from those with one week before their test, to those with less than a week, and for those who aren't sure … or can't remember.

Additives like Urine Luck and Tinkle Sprinkle are now easily detected in analysis, even if you do successfully get them into the sample. For those faced with utterly random testing, therefore, the only viable option is said to be urine substitution – and in order to allow you to heat it to body temperature, and to conceal it on your person, you might try 'The Clean Machine Urine Substitution System', a kit containing enough real human urine for two tests, in frozen form (no mixing, but needs to be thawed with hot water a few hours before, so is less portable) or dehydrated (distilled water must be added, but it is completely portable), certified drug-free and vacuum-sealed for an extended one-year shelf-life; a heating element to maintain the right temperature; or an adjustable belt for observed testing.

Prescriptive

On the outer fringes of the broad blanket of urine testing are the 'nutripathic' tests hawked by nutritionists as the basis for evaluating someone's health and prescribing dietary supplements to fix their problems. Some claim miracle nutritional programmes for HIV and cancer, or products that block absorption of fats and carbohydrates; others market their wares as a sideline to non-accredited correspondence schools that grant 'degrees' in nutrition, with brochures that scream their phoniness on every line: nutripathy is 'the condensation of most all natural healing and counseling techniques available today … the basics 'boiled' from literally hundreds of different therapies and techniques' – into a meaningless mush. A basic kit might cost $280 and promise to 'determine up to 2,600 different health conditions by analyzing chemical, digestive and nutritional imbalances within the body.'

Tellingly, many of these practitioners demand the completion of 'informed consent' forms by their clients, to agree that their urine and saliva specimens are screenings for research purposes only – and that they will never take legal action against the nutritionist.

Eight

From Alchemy to Chemistry

Alchemists of the middle ages and later were obsessed by transmutation, especially the possibility of changing other metals into gold. They were interested in urine for various reasons, including the fact that it came out of the body and was yellow, roughly the same colour as gold. Many alchemists and early chemists worked with urine, including Robert Boyle, but the most important discovery was made in 1669 by Hennig Brandt. He evaporated urine, heated the residue with powdered charcoal and condensed the vapour that came off. The result was a snow-white waxy solid that caught fire immediately, producing a dark and choking smoke, but then glowed in the dark, without heat; he could read his old alchemist's tomes by its light. He christened this substance phosphorus (Greek for 'light-bearer') – a name which it shares with the planet Venus as morning star. Phosphorus was a new element, and its discovery was a stepping stone to the newborn subject of chemistry.

Boyle improved the recipe, and was the first not only systemically to examine the properties of this 'icy noctiluca' (cold light), but also to use phosphorus to ignite sulphur-tipped wooden splints, the very earliest sort of matchstick. From urine had flowed not gold, but, in the shape of a new chemical element (the first ever to be isolated by experiment), a white light, a golden fire.

William Y-Worth, repeating Brandt's work, described the preparation in detail, and added the cautionary note about phosphorus, 'If the Privy Parts be therewith rubb'd, they will be inflamed and burning for a good while after.' Don't try this at home!

The First Chemical Industry

The discovery of phosphorus seems to signal the transition from alchemy to chemistry, but in fact a substantial chemical industry had already been established on the north coast of Yorkshire in the early 1600s. The story began with the marital problems of Henry VIII and the Tudors' subsequent inability to dye effectively.

Most Tudor clothes were made of wool and coloured with vegetable dyes – you can make a fine yellow dye from onion skins, for example. However, if you just dip the wool into a solution of dye the colour is not very bright, and it soon washes out, because it is not fast. What you need is a chemical called a mordant, which, from the Latin, means one that can bite into the fibres of the wool and into the molecules of the dye and so bind them together.

The best mordant at the time was alum, a mineral that came from the Tolfa Hills near Rome. In about 1530, however, Henry VIII announced that he wanted to divorce his first wife, Catherine of Aragon, which sparked off a tremendous row with the pope. The Vatican cut off the supply of alum, so the British could no longer dye their cloth; it all had to be sent to Flanders, where it was badly dyed at great expense. So the hunt was on to find alum in Britain, and prospectors searched far and wide – but had no luck even in such promising places as Alum Chine in Dorset and Alum Bay on the Isle of Wight.

Then, about the year 1600, Thomas Challoner seems to have brought back from the continent an extraordinary recipe that allowed the Britons to make their own alum. They dug grey shale from the cliffs on the north Yorkshire coast, roasted it over a slow fire for nine months, washed the residue with water and to the washings added stale human urine. They warmed the liquid in great lead pans until a fresh chicken's egg just floated to the surface, which was a signal that the concentration was optimal. Then they left the solution to cool, and great crystals of pure alum grew on the sides and bottom of the containers. With this alum they were at last able to dye their clothes.

The chemistry is quite subtle. The shale contains aluminium oxide combined with other minerals, and also iron sulphide. The slow roasting causes oxidation of the sulphide to sulphate, and aluminium sulphate can be washed out of the ash – but if the fire is too fierce the sulphur is all burned off as sulphur dioxide, and there is none left to make sulphate.

Aluminium sulphate is a good mordant, but is hard to purify; it is usually contaminated with iron salts, which spoil the colour. This is where the stale urine comes in. As urine decomposes, it forms ammonia, and the staler it is the more ammonia accumulates in the liquid. The ammonia combines with the crude aluminium sulphate to make the double salt ammonium aluminium sulphate, which is the chemical name for alum, and alum is easy to crystallize and purify. Other forms of alum contain potassium or sodium instead of ammonium, but these do not need urine.

Legend had it that the best urine came from poor working people who did not consume so much strong drink, but it is unlikely that this was ever tested, since urine from dozens if not hundreds of people was all mixed together. In the early days the urine was collected from the local farms, where barrels were provided for all the men, but demand exceeded supply, and soon urine had to be shipped to North Yorkshire from Newcastle and from Hull where, allegedly, the first ever public lavatories were installed just to collect the vital ingredient. When further supplies were needed they were brought from London. Buckets were placed on street corners for men to contribute; every week a horse came round with barrels to collect the stuff, like a milk round in reverse; and the barrels were taken to the docks and shipped up the North Sea to the port of Whitby.

The quantities of urine are astonishing. In the last two months of 1612 alone, 16,000 gallons of 'country urine' and 13,000 gallons of London urine were taken from Whitby to the alum works at Sandsend, a couple of miles north. This was a lucrative business for the ship owners. Records show that coal was shipped from Newcastle and Sunderland to Whitby, from where alum would be shipped to London, and that the ships would return sloshing with urine. Master Luke Fox, Whitby mariner, took twenty-three tonnes of urine to Whitby, and returned to London with twenty-nine tonnes of alum.

One story goes that the skippers of these ships were embarrassed at their increasingly smelly cargo, and that when asked what they were carrying they would say it was wine, to which the smart response was 'Oh no – you're taking the piss.' And it is possible that this is the origin of that expression (see also page 109).

How on earth did they discover this extraordinary process? Can you imagine someone digging a lump of shale from the cliff, roasting it for nine months and then pissing on it, just to see what happened? Nevertheless, someone somewhere did stumble on it, and eventually a great industry grew up along the cliffs for 15 miles either side of Whitby. Millions of tonnes of shale were hacked our of the cliffs – you can see the quarries today, from Boulby to Ravenscar – and hundreds of men worked for some 250 years in the first major chemical industry, all based on stale human urine.

Urine was used in various other ways in dyeing: it helped prepare the wool for the dye to take, and it was also used in the preparation of the dyes themselves. A seventeenth-century recipe for indigo reads, 'Take 12 gallons of chamber lye … sett it on the fire; then when it is almost boiling, take the scum clean off it and then take it off the fire, and let it settle … take a quarter of a pound of indigo, mingle them together, then take your cloth or wool … and stir them verie well about.' The indigo would be imported from the Near East, where for centuries the dark blue pigment had been extracted from cut and dried indigo plants by being fermented in urine in the hot sun for several days.

Other Applications of Stale Urine

In a discreet corner of my garden is a straw-bale urinal – a small straw bale stuffed into a plastic box with the cut ends of the straw uppermost. I regularly pee in it and encourage other members of the family and visitors to do so too. The urine disappears into the straw without a splash. The bale does not smell, but after a few months the urine will have decomposed inside to leave a brown crumbly centre. This is rich in ammonia, and is an excellent fertiliser – it can go straight on the compost heap or the freshly dug soil. Gardeners used to swear by urine for swelling carrots, celery, tomatoes and rhubarb, and the finest lawns were dressed with urine to promote the green colour.

Plants need the element nitrogen in order to make proteins, and the best source of nitrogen is ammonia. Therefore urinating in a water closet and flushing it away is a waste of good nitrogen that could feed the plants in the garden. Another effective way of retaining the nitrogen is to pee directly on to the compost heap – but not on to the plants, for the concentration is too high, and the urine can 'burn' the vegetation (see also Family Pets ..., pages 157–160).

Animal urine also decomposes to produce ammonia, and in hot places this may be further oxidised to nitrate, especially potassium nitrate, or saltpetre. For hundreds of years the best sources of this were the animal sheds in India and other hot countries, where crystals of saltpetre could simply be scraped off the walls. Saltpetre became immensely important in the manufacture of gunpowder, which is roughly 75 per cent saltpetre, with 15 per cent charcoal and 10 per cent sulphur.

Because decomposing urine contains ammonia, it has been used in all sorts of ways in which ammonia is used today: as a bleach, for cleaning everything from saucepans to hair, in cheese-making, and in curing leather and even tobacco. Hair was also often bleached by washing in urine and then drying in the sun.

Stale urine or lye was always used in the fulling process for preparing raw wool, which comes off the sheep greasy and dirty. The wool was placed in a tub of fermenting urine, and the fullers would stamp about on it with bare feet, to work the liquid into the fibres of the cloth. Because it is alkaline, the ammonia in the stale urine helps to remove the grease and the dirt, and leaves the wool much softer and easier to spin and to weave. Subsequent rinsing in clean water removes both the residue from the grease and any surplus urine. As late as 1935 a mill near Huddersfield was still using urine for scouring the wool, and the staff were expected to contribute generously.

Surprisingly, urine found various uses in heavy industry well into the twentieth century. It was a lubricant in the process of wire drawing, for lubricating the big ends of engines, and for hardening such tools as chisels and hammerheads; horse or goat urine was specially recommended for producing good hard steel.

Urine was so useful in so many industries that it was often a handy source of income for the poor. It was normally worth a penny a bucket, or half as much again for redheads. The average family could therefore earn sixpence a week, which was enough for a good meal. The Roman emperor Vespasian even slapped a tax on urine. His son protested, but Vespasian held a coin under his nose and asked, 'Does it smell?' In Paris the French honoured him by calling their pissoirs *vespasiennes*.

Urine also has a long history of use as invisible ink. Pee into a cup or bottle, dip a toothpick or other pen in it, and write your message. Once it is dry it is invisible, but the residue turns brown when it is gently heated – for example using an ordinary light bulb. During World War II an intelligence officer called Charles Fraser-Smith made all sorts of James-Bond-type gadgets, including miniature cameras and compasses, and handkerchiefs that when you peed on them turned into maps of the area. He called them his wee maps.

Nine

Urban Myths

Urine stars in a number of colourful myths, featuring Coke cans, swimming pools, subway lines and sharp-toothed fishes.

In the Red

Kids believe that a special compound added to the water in swimming pools will reveal the presence of urine. The chemical industry can issue all the denials it likes – the childish certainty (and the lingering adult fear) persists that a surreptitious piss will spread a great red or purple cloud of incrimination around the weak-willed or weak-bladdered culprit. To make such a specific dye would be exceedingly difficult – and there is no need. Though we don't like to think of it, a little healthy urine in our highly chlorinated baths is harmless – and imagine the temptation for mischievous kids to fill the water with colourful trails, if the myth became reality. While it remains in the realm of whispered surmise, however, it remains an effective way for parents to keep their kids under control.

Swimming Against the Stream

There is, they say, a fish that can swim up the flow of piss into the urethra of one who pees unawares in a tropical river, even while standing, and easily while bathing. It is often then reported to force itself into the innermost passages of the body by following the trail of urine, there to glut itself on mucous membranes and tissues till internal bleeding drowns it or kills its host. Some of these fish have the added refinement of spreading themselves umbrella-like once they've reached the urethra, meaning you can't pull them out even if you do catch them by the tail. Impromptu surgery is said to be the lesser of available agonies.

One of the most popular identities found for the fish is the candirú (*Vandellia cirrhosa*) of the Amazon, a three-inch-long, fast-swimming slimy catfish with sharp teeth and streamlined spines which, though it is not known to be specifically urinophilic, is known to lodge in the gills of larger fish, there to feed on the blood of its host. But tales of its squirming its way into human crevices — one report says women, having a larger aperture, are more at risk — seem highly improbable, and rely on sources from the 1930s and '40s, which themselves rely on second- and third-hand evidence from missionaries, doctors and natives. One piece of the latter sort suggests a typical twisting of half-relevant fact to fit the fiction: Amazon tribes use the green fruit of the jagua tree (*Genipa americana L.*) to make a tea which, when drunk hot, is said to dissolve the fish's bones and eject it from the body in a matter of hours; a urologist in the mid-Forties reported, however, that a synthetic version of this brew had dissolved bladder 'incrustations' and might act similarly on kidney stones – so suggesting that this remedy got rid of unidentified internal problems rather than fish skeletons.

Live Rail

A different sort of death by urine is more cosmopolitan: a drunkard taking the subway home pees on the tracks and is electrocuted when his urine hits the live rail. This is possible in theory – urine, as a solution of salts in water, is a good conductor of electricity, and will transmit the current; but to pee that far and with such good – or bad – aim would be quite a feat for the soberest of men.

Water Intake

A less dramatic destruction might itself be wreaked by the supposedly health-giving regime of drinking eight glasses/two litres of water a day. The healthiness of this, some say, is a myth propagated by the bottled-water sellers to keep us drinking before we're thirsty. Critics say that the body's osmoregulatory system, in the form of the antidiuretic hormone and simple thirst (which begins when the concentration of the blood has risen by less than two per cent, where dehydration doesn't kick in till about five per cent – a healthy safety margin), is perfectly adept at maintaining water balance. And although drinking lots while exercising or in extreme heat is essential regardless of thirst, some athletes and clubbers have experienced mental confusion, even died, after drinking simply too much – succumbing to 'water intoxication', where the kidneys just can't get rid of enough water.

The notion that dark urine means dehydration is also overly simplistic. The colour varies inversely with the volume, and the volume in turn varies greatly from one person to the next. So water should not perhaps remain the failsafe elixir of the health- and figure-conscious. Not only does a high water intake increase the risk of exposure to pollutants, severely deplete the

bank balance of those who insist on the stylish bottled sort
and induce feelings of guilt and inadequacy in those who fail
to reach their daily liquid targets, but it multiplies the amount
of urinating you'll have to do, with all the inconvenience and
embarrassment that frequent pee-stops bring. So lurking in
here somewhere is either a scientific maxim that ought to
be considered a myth, or a myth-hungry attack on sensible
science …

Rat Pee

A final and comparatively colourless legend – also more a
health scare than a myth – is that rat urine is toxic to humans
– and, moreover, that almost every soft drinks can is encrusted
with it. Unnamed 'studies' reveal that Spanish drinks cans are
more bacteria-laden than public loos. 'Friend of a family friend'
tales of death by a few hapless swigs of fizzy orange abound,
peopled with images of rodent-infested warehouses where
cans languish for month upon neglected month. 'All those
people who drink straight from the can' are urged to spread the
altruistic word: 'we need to be more careful everywhere.'

Some of the deaths turn out to be of leptospirosis, or Weil's
Disease – which can lead to anything from aches and pains and
fever, through jaundice and meningitis and internal bleeding
and kidney failure, to death. The urine of a healthy rat is no
more inherently toxic than that of any other animal; the stories
take their modicum of truth from the fact that rats (amongst
other animals) infected with leptospirosis can pass the disease

on to humans through their urine (or other bodily fluids). But sipping from fizzy drinks cans is a far less likely medium of infection than drinking contaminated water, or letting it touch an open cut, or even splashing through puddles and rubbing the eyes. Most cans are packaged in cardboard boxes on the production line, and transported with all possible speed to the buyer, before the fizz begins to fade; and if rats are hanging out in the bottling plant, they'll be peeing near where they're living, near where they're finding their food – which will be not a deserted warehouse, but where product ingredients are mixed, or, better, where workers are taking their lunch breaks. Shiny can tops might look like attractive rat loos to us, but if there are no dining facilities close by, the rats won't be interested. Wipe your can if you like – but the greater dangers you'll be cleaning off will be from human hands, not rodent genitals.

Ten

Politics and Psychology

The International Centre for Bathroom Etiquette (ICBE) takes this matter pretty seriously. 'At the ICBE we work hard every day to bring you the latest in cutting edge research on bathroom etiquette. Our mission is simple and our goals are clear: Educate everyone on proper bathroom conduct, and in so doing make the bathroom experience more enjoyable for everyone.' Their FAQ list covers such topics as Talking in the Bathroom, Bathrooms Equipped with Troughs, Stalls without Walls, Kiddie-Sized Urinals, Urinals with Partitions, Hanging the Toilet Paper, Which Sink to Use, What if you have to Pee *Really* Badly, and Those One-Person Bathrooms; but most endearingly, heading the list, is 'Why?'

The Original Guide to Urinal Etiquette (including tips on how to deal with all the ramifications of urinal occupancy – The Ideal Situation, Two Urinal Tango, Three's Company, etc.) is eerily reminiscent of the Urinal Game (see pages 37–38), except that here learning definitely comes before fun. Even the merchandise page keeps frivolity at bay: 'Have you ever wanted a fancy ICBE t-shirt? What about a cool ICBE mug? Well even if you haven't, that shouldn't stop you from visiting our online store! Pick something up to help support our global research efforts.'

Pre-empting accusations of sexism, they confess that they're 'Looking for a Female Etiquette Correspondent: Do you know what goes on in women's bathrooms? Well we don't, so if you do, we want to hear from you! Take a look at the heavy male bias on our staff page, and you'll get a pretty quick idea of what the problem is. We are recruiting female etiquette correspondents to join our cause and fight for good bathroom behaviour and etiquette across the globe!' Finally, they direct us to other realms of internet delight, including BathroomLife.com, Restrooms.org, UrineSurvey.com – and Urinal.net.

Personal Space

In the West we regard excretion as something private. The only general exception to this is the men's urinal, where men pee together standing in rows. So how embarrassed are men when they have to urinate standing next to someone else? Now we know, thanks to the pioneering work of American psychologists R. Dennis Middlemist and his colleagues, who found that the fewer people are around, the quicker men start peeing and the longer they go on. Having someone close by delays the start (see page 120) and reduces the peeing time.

First they did a pilot study, simply observing men come into the gents in a university building. A man pretending to groom himself at the mirror noted which stall the subject occupied, whether there was anyone nearby, how long it took him to start peeing after unzipping, and how long he peed for. They measured these times with a stopwatch by listening to the stream, since there was water in the urinals, and the urine fell audibly.

Forty-eight urinators were observed, none of whom took a stall next to one already occupied. The average delay time before the 'onset of micturation' was 5.7 seconds when there was no one within two stalls, 5.9 seconds when there was someone two stalls away, and 7.9 seconds when the next stall but one was occupied. The corresponding 'micturation persistences' were 32.0 seconds, 24.4 seconds, and 19.0 seconds.

Encouraged by this trial run, Middlemist and company set out to do some serious research, in another Gents' on campus. Sixty men were watched, without being told they were part of an experiment. This time there was no water in the urinals, so the observer had to hide in a cubicle and watch the subjects with a periscope.

All the subjects were forced to use the left-hand of three adjacent stalls, either alone, or with a stooge in the right-hand one, or with a stooge in the centre; the stooges were colleagues of the researchers. The other stalls were barred by notices saying Do Not Use and had buckets underneath. The stalls were of generous proportions – 18 inches wide with 18 inches between them.

This time the results were unchallengeable. The micturation delay increased from an average of 4.9 seconds when the subject was alone, to 6.2 seconds with someone one stall away, to 8.4 seconds with someone next door, while the persistence dropped from 24.8 seconds to 23.4 seconds to 17.4 seconds.

The conclusion? Close interpersonal distances are stressful and increase arousal and discomfort; arousal causes delay, and shortens performance. The researchers suggested that the effects of intravesical pressure (pressure in the bladder) could be better estimated from the volume of urine excreted. So if you see a group of psychologists lurking in the Gents' with measuring jugs you will know what they are doing! The Urinal Game was right about that indispensable 'buffer zone' (see page 37).

To Sit or to Stand?

Pissing becomes a highly politicised matter for people whose sex and gender also are. Female-to-male transsexuals are unlikely to procure the whole apparatus for peeing standing up, but many male-to-females have their whole penis cut off – but then get traumatized by being unable to 'perform' – not in the bedroom, but in the restroom. The web is peppered with advice on how to pee standing without a penis – and on how to pee in the stall without too openly declaring oneself a 'weirdo' or a 'sissy' – this from those who defiantly protest that the right to sit is any (wo)man's. It's funny that this has become such emotive territory, though, for what seem biologically imperative opposites are only cultural conventions determined by time and place: in many Muslim countries both men and women squat (to avoid the potential for unclean spatterings); in Bolivia, the women's stiff multi-layered skirts allow them the same freedoms men have; while some Native American men would squat and their women stand. In nineteenth-century Switzerland old women reportedly stood too ... Finally, there are those who through vanity or the quest for sexual ecstasy find themselves forced daily to make more of a sexual statement than they'd anticipated: men who go for penis piercings may have misgivings when they find themselves dribbling piss from their new holes on to the urinal floor – and reading surreptitiously all the advice on discreet cubicle use.

Political Ambiguity

A once common sign in public lavatories, on trains, was GENTLEMEN PLEASE LIFT THE SEAT. Perhaps lower classes were not expected to carry out this complex operation ... In his trouser-monologue during the 1961 satirical revue *Beyond the fringe*, Jonathan Miller made some more detailed suggestions: 'that marvellous unpunctuated motto over lavatory saying GENTLEMEN LIFT THE SEAT. What exactly does it mean? Is it a sociological description – a definition of a gentleman which I can either take or leave? Or perhaps it's a Loyal Toast? It could be a blunt military order ... or an invitation to upper-class larceny ...'

Piss in Peace

One solution to that eternal well-spring of domestic strife, the toilet-lid, might be the home urinal. And indeed reports from the United States suggest that it's a growing trend, particularly among households with young sons or laddish husbands (a Mr Jones recalls the reaction from his high-fiving buddies: 'You got a urinal. Awesome! How'd you talk your wife into that?'); celebrity converts include Black Sabbath 'Prince of Darkness' turned domestic-'reality'-TV-star Ozzy Osbourne. Proud owners quickly start to sound like vintage car enthusiasts: one satisfied customer gushes that 'She is a

1983 Eljer with a chrome-on-brass 1968 Haws freeze-resistant flush valve ... which has been in service since 1991 when I recycled her'; urinals also provide endless amusement for the DIY enthusiast.

The J.L. Mott Iron Works in New York may have been the original trendsetters: in 1888 they offered a little more domesticity with their porcelain-lined foldable version, explaining in their catalogue that 'It has been our desire for many years to get a urinal ... that would be adapted for private use in all rooms set aside for gentlemen's use, such as billiard and smoking rooms, private offices, etc.' Resistance has remained to the idea of allowing such a potent symbol of masculinity into the home, let alone the feminine sanctuary that is so often the bathroom; but now there's a hunger for 'conversation pieces' – and what else could you call a floor-length fixture in its own alcove, with tiled classical vaulting? One home-design company has blamed the name for putting female clients off, and started to call the urinal a 'rose' – leaving salesmen free then to extol its virtues: how it saves water (especially the no-flush variety) and lets you put in a plush carpet ...

Urinal Ingenuity

Some urinals politely refuse to flush until the user has actually urinated, making life difficult for pre-flushers. Such men are a source of common mockery and infuriation – is their pee too pure to be mixed with whatever lower-caste urine might have been there before; are they pretending they're peeing into a waterfall? But could you stomach a urinal that asks in imperturbably dulcet tones, 'Are you sure you want to flush? You haven't begun to urinate yet. Remember, water is a precious resource. (Guilt-inducing pause.) If you must flush now, pull the handle again within three seconds, or just begin urinating like a normal person. Thank you.'

A headrest above the urinal or the conventional lavatory would be a kinder addition to the apparatus of piss, for the time when the evening's drawing on, and the eyes are a little blurry with beer – what a pleasure to sink one's forehead into cushiony softness for a minute before rejoining the throng. What's more, it would improve the angle of the body, and so minimize dribbling over the edge. And then, for the ultimate male luxury, a urinal set into the shower, to solve forever that tricky dilemma, 'Should I pee first and then shower? Shower then pee? Pee down the drain?' Add a 'wet bar' and you'd never have to leave …

For those who suffer from 'shy-bladder syndrome' (perhaps including some of the pre-flushers above), headphones playing a recording of babbling brooks would be a less wasteful option than keeping real water running. Knowing that babies and horses can be induced to urinate by the sound of running water, Dr Reese Alsop found this also worked for many of his patients who, after operations, had difficulty starting. He had been especially worried about those in intensive care – catheters are uncomfortable and undignified, and often lead to infection; so he made a thirty-minute tape from a sound-effects library, with 'a rich medley of aquatic phonetics. Splashing, gurgling, lapping, running, roaring, dripping, flushing sounds follow in easy sequence.' He made the tape available in the hospital, and found it effective in sixty out of eighty patients. He warned, however, that earphones are vital; on one or two occasions the audio catheter was inadvertently beamed to an audience greater than one. Both nursing staff and patients in neighbouring beds complained that it was highly effective!

Happily, Tokyo-based toilet manufacturers Toto now provide a model with inbuilt sound system, playing watery noises in the interests of the many self-conscious Japanese who flush excessively to mask the sound once they have started – though it could just as well be adopted by all those who can't start.

Even legends of beauty and tragedy are not immune to the awkward acoustics of pissing. While Marilyn Monroe was engaged to Arthur Miller, she went to meet his mother at her tiny New York apartment, whose walls were so paper-thin that when Marilyn went to pee she was scared her tinkling would be heard, and turned on all the taps to mask the sound. When Miller rang the day after for his mother's verdict, she replied: 'She's sweet. A wonderful girl. But she pisses like a horse!'

Pee on a Bee

Urinal design seems to be coming full circle: in the early days, gentlemen unfamiliar with the concept of such directional excretion would aim towards a 'pissing point' on the porcelain – a small illustration of a bee (the Latin for bee being 'apis'). Today the outlines of flies are appearing etched into the porcelain of public urinals, notably those of Amsterdam's

Schiphol airport, where informal studies have shown they reduce spillage by eighty per cent. This Dutch 'technology' is now to be transferred to New York's JFK airport, though a spokesperson for the former mayor Guiliani is said to have retorted: 'What do we need with Dutch flies when we have more than enough roaches to piss on?'

In Britain we've so far just hoped that asking politely will do the trick: signs in the Gents in pubs sometimes read: WE AIM TO PLEASE – YOU AIM TOO, PLEASE.

Pissing for Victory

Pissing is a powerful weapon of war, as action and as rhetoric: the US Army General George S. Patton, known for his extreme toughness, his discipline and his self-sacrifice, and nick-named 'Old Blood-and-Guts', stopped on 24 March 1945 to urinate in the middle of one of the newly-constructed and strategically crucial pontoon bridges over the Rhine. He is reported to have sent the following communiqué to Eisenhower: 'Dear SHAEF [Supreme Allied Commander of the Allied Expeditionary Force], I have just pissed into the Rhine River. For God's sake, send some gasoline.' (The striking photographic evidence was later doctored by Army censors to remove the urine stream.)

He was known, too, for his profane eloquence, his speeches dotted with expletives that always seemed to belong there: asked about this by his nephew, Patton remarked that 'When I want my men to remember something important, to really make it stick, I give it to them double dirty. It may not sound nice to some bunch of little old ladies at an afternoon tea party, but it helps my soldiers to remember. You can't run an army without profanity; and it has to be eloquent profanity. An army without profanity couldn't fight its way out of a piss-soaked paper bag.'

For less conventional combatants, too, piss is a form of defiance – if only dreamt-of. On 10 November 1972 two men hijacked Southern Airways flight 49 out of Birmingham, Alabama, and sent it careering over the US, to Canada and to Cuba, while making their demand for seven million dollars. They circled the top-secret nuclear installation at the Oak Ridge National Laboratory, Tennessee, and threatened to crash the plane there. But when two days had elapsed and most of the mini alcohol bottles were drained, they landed it in Havana, to be jailed by Castro. One of them later proclaimed, unrepentant: 'I wanted to fly over the Statue of Liberty and urinate on it.'

Pee Springs Eternal

Urine has been used to quench the most symbolic of fires: on 2 July, during the 1998 World Cup, Mexican football fan Rodrigo Rafael Ortega extinguished the seventy-seven-year-old 'eternal flame' that burns at the Arc de Triomphe on the grave of an unknown WWI soldier – by drunkenly pissing on it. He was arrested, for 'offending the dead' and being drunk in public – and treated for minor burns to his bottom. The French junior minister for war veterans, Jean-Pierre Masseret, declared, 'We are deeply hurt by this unspeakable act'; a statement by the

Defence Ministry said the flame had been 'soiled'; 'This has been an attack on the memory of those who died for France, and their honour.' The flame was relit days later, and Mexico's ambassador to France laid a wreath at its foot. The previous year an Australian had been arrested for trying to cook an egg on the flame; and in January 2002 an unnamed French soldier who tried to emulate the beer-bloated Mexican was arrested and sent to a mental institution.

Eleven

Language

The word 'piss' was considered Standard English until Victorian prudes declared it a vulgarism. It appeared in 1290 in *The South English Legendary*, which describes a man's call of nature as the time 'when he would [i.e. wanted to] piss'. It comes from the Vulgar Latin imitative 'pissiare', via the Old Frisian 'pissia' – leading also to the French 'pisser'. Indeed, it seems to have been one of the Indo-European words that bridged all boundaries: the Middle Dutch and Middle Low German had 'pissen'; the Danish was 'pissa'; Swedish, Norwegian, and Icelandic 'pyssa'; Welsh 'piso' or 'pisio'; and similar forms exist in Italian and Romanian.

According to the *Oxford English Dictionary*, the word piss is no longer in polite use, and so people have come up with a flood of supposedly more polite expressions.

Euphemisms in Cockney Rhyming Slang

Ken Smee	pee
Arthur Bliss	piss (in Australian rhyming slang, 'Johnny Bliss')
gypsy's kiss	piss e.g. 'Just going for a gypsy's – back in a mo'
hit and miss	piss (also kiss)
jimmy riddle	an act of urination; rhyming slang for 'piddle'; often split up into just 'jimmy', or 'riddle'
snake's hiss	piss e.g. 'Just popping in for a quick snake's'
Brahms and Liszt	pissed (drunk)
Oliver Twist	pissed (drunk)
Schindler's List	pissed (drunk), e.g. 'Down the pub, getting Schindler's …'
Scotch mist	pissed (drunk)

Other Euphemisms for Piss and Pissing

bleed/leak the lizard

call of nature – the need to urinate (or defecate) (as early as 1540, the term 'nature' was linked to the need to go to the privy; in Lord Chesterfield's *Letters* of 1747 an elegant accumulation of euphemism describes 'that small portion of [time] which the calls of nature obliged him to pass in the necessary-house'; today we might excuse ourselves with the snappier 'nature calls')

change the water on the goldfish

do number one – e.g. 'Me want do numma one'

do one's business – to urinate (or defecate) (since the following recorded use in 1645, in a propaganda pamphlet, the *Sacred Decretal or Hue and Cry for the Apprehension of Martin Mar-Priest*: 'have [...] a care [...] that no birds build, chatter, or do their business or sing there'

drain down the system

drain the main vein (of males)

drain the one-eyed monster

drain the radiator

freshen one's Snapple

go to water one's horse

leak – e.g. 'Hold on a minute, I need to take a leak.'

break the seal

lower the water level

my back teeth are floating/afloat – expression of an intense need to pee, obsolete in Britain by 1960, surviving longer in the US

pass water – the phrase was originally 'make water'. The 1535 Coverdale version of the Bible has 2 Kings 9:8 as 'I will root out from Ahab even him that maketh water against the wall, (see also page 44); it also has the French equivalent, still in use: 'faire de l'eau' pee (verb/noun) – a simple shortening of the word 'piss', attested from 1788

piddle (verb/noun)

plant/do a sweet pea – to urinate, especially outdoors (since the nineteenth century, used of and by women; an earlier version, meaning to go to the loo more generally, is 'to pluck a rose', as most rural privies were in the garden)

point the pink pistol (or Percy) at the porcelain/punish the porcelain (male usage)

powder one's nose – used to excuse oneself from company (female usage)

pump ship – since 1788, originally sailors' slang for either urinating or vomiting; a century later it had been adopted as a gentleman's colloquialism; it draws on both naval and plumbing terms, as do its more vulgar equivalents, 'to spring a leak' and 'take a leak'

refresh the body

release the pressure

relieve/ease oneself, give oneself ease – to urinate (or defecate) (the sense of 'to relieve' as giving a person or part of the body ease from physical pain or discomfort was common by 1375; by 1842 the association had become more specific, with a treatise on *Physiological Digestion* declaring that 'bowels act to relieve the system')

see a man about a horse/dog (male usage)

shake hands with the unemployed (male usage)

shake the dew off the lily – from about 1930, possibly Irish in origin siphon the python

sis-sis, cis-cis/sissy, cissy (noun)

slash – e.g. 'take/go for a slash'

spend a penny – originates from the door lock on a cubicle in a
  public lavatory, opened by inserting a penny – as pioneered
  in 1851 (see page 17)

sprinkle

steer Stanley to the stainless steel (male usage)

strain the potatoes

take/make a pit stop

tap a keg – US, equating the bladder with a beer keg; also 'to
  go tap a kidney'

tea (noun) – originally British, coined as early as 1716,
  when John Gay noted with irritation in his *Trivia* that
  'thoughtless wits […] 'gainst [the] Sentry's Box discharge
  their tea'; it may come from the similar colour of the two
  liquids, or from the rhyme, or from tea's diuretic effect

tinkle (verb/noun) – originally US

water the garden/tulips/tomatoes

wazz – e.g. 'go for a wazz'

wee (-wee)

whiz (noun) – from the hissing sound, related to 'wheeze,'
  from Old Norse 'hvaesa', to hiss

Sexual Practices

golden shower – an act of urinating on another for sexual pleasure

watersports (or water sports) – the practice of urinating on another for the sexual pleasure of both parties

Proverbs and Words of Wisdom

The urine of one dog will not pollute the ocean. (French)

All skill is in vain when an angel pees in the touchhole of your musket. (German)

Pee on the ruins before they build a temple over them. (Sicilian)

A rich man has a canopy over his head. A poor man has a can o' pee under his bed.

Jokes

Why did the blonde pee in the grocery store? Because the sign said 'Wet Floor'.

Why did Captain Kirk piss on the roof of the Enterprise? To boldly go where no man has gone before.

A famous music-hall song opened, 'She sits among the cabbages and peas.' The Lord Chancellor took exception and banned the song. So the singer revised the words and sang, 'She sits among the cabbages and leeks.'

Three old men are sitting on a porch. 'I wish I could take a healthy piss,' says one. 'I wish I could take a healthy crap,' says the second. 'I can take a crap at 6 am and a piss at 11 am,' says the third; 'I just wish I could get up before noon.'

Harvard and Yale graduates meet in a washroom during a law convention, and the Yale grad goes to leave without washing his hands. The Harvard man says, 'Didn't they teach you to wash your hands at Yale?' The Yale man answers, 'They taught us not to piss on our hands.'

Two men out fishing find a lamp in the water. One of them picks it up and rubs it, and a genie appears. Unfortunately, it's a low-level genie, and can grant only one wish. The men think for a few minutes and then wish for the entire lake to be made of beer. With a *Poof!* the wish is granted, but then one of the men exclaims, 'Dammit! Now we have to piss in the boat!'

Early one morning the President looks out of the White House window, and sees 'The President Sucks' written in the snow with urine. Furious, he calls in the FBI and demands that they find the perpetrators. Later that day the FBI agent returns. 'Well sir, the urine has been analysed and it's the Vice-President's.' The President goes purple with rage and shouts, 'Is that all?' 'Well no sir,' says the agent, 'The handwriting is the First Lady's.'

For ten dollars and a urine sample, a machine in the pharmacy claims to tell you what is wrong with you. A man with a sore elbow puts in his ten dollars and his urine sample; a minute later the diagnosis comes out: he has tennis elbow, and he should soak it in warm water. Convinced the machine must be a fraud, he devises a scheme to fool it. He makes a mixture of his daughter's urine, his dog's urine and his own semen, and puts that in with ten dollars. The diagnosis? 'The dog has worms, your daughter is on drugs, and she's not your daughter.'

A drinker says to the bartender, 'Betcha $100 if you put a whisky glass on that end of the bar, and I stood on this end, I could piss into it and not spill a drop.' The bartender eagerly takes the bet, knowing he can't lose. The man climbs unsteadily on to the bar, unzips his fly and pisses all over the bar. The bartender laughs and says, 'You owe me $100.' The man pays the money with a big smile on his face. The bartender asks, 'How come you're so happy?' 'Well,' says the man, 'I bet those guys over there $200 that I could piss all over your bar and you'd laugh about it.'

Note: This must be read with an Italian accent, preferably out loud. Lasta year I wenna Malta to a bigga hotel. Ina morning I go to eata brekfast. I tella waitress I wanna two pissis toast. She brings me only one piss. I tella her I want two piss. She says go to the toilet. I say you no understand. I wanna two piss onna my plate. She say you better not not piss on plate you sonna ma bitch. Later I go to eat at the bigga restaurant. The waitress brings me a spoon and knife but no fock. I tella her I wanna fock. She

tell me everyone does. I tella her you no understand, I wanna
fock on the table. She say better not fock on table, you sonna
ma bitch. I don't even know the lady and she call me a sonna
ma bitch. So I go to my room inna hotel, and there is no sheit.
I call the manager and tella him I wanna a sheit. He tella me go
to the toilet. I say you no understand, I wanna sheit on my bed.
He say you better not sheit on bed you sonna ma bitch. I don't
even know the man and he call me a sonna ma bitch. I go to the
checkout and the man at the desk say: 'Peace unto you.' I say,
'Piss unto you too, ya sonna ma bitch. I gonna back to Italy.'

Slang

full of piss and vinegar – lively, full of vim and vigour (this
   phrase makes perhaps its first recorded appearance in
   Steinbeck's 1938 *The Grapes of Wrath*: "'How ya keepin'
   yaself?' "Full a piss an' vinegar."' – and since it stands there
   without explanation, it must already have been in common
   parlance. It appears frequently thereafter, right up to Bart's
   1994 declaration in the Simpsons – "'I'm full of piss and
   vinegar."')

full of piss and wind – full of blustering talk, pretentious
   (dates to 1922)

pee it down – to rain heavily

Peedy Gonzalez – a person, especially a woman, who does not
   travel to the loo in a group but instead pees quickly, washes
   her hands, and returns, ruining everyone's chance to talk
   behind her back (from the Looney Tunes cartoon character
   Speedy Gonzalez)

pididdle – to creatively expend time and energy doing what appears to have no real-world value to anyone (including yourself), and to have a good time doing it e.g. 'I'm pididdling my way through the real reasons dragons can fly despite being so large and heavy.'

piece of piss – something very easy

pish down – to rain heavily (Scottish)

pished – drunk, intoxicated (Scottish)

piss – 1. a weak drink; 2. beer (Australian) e.g. 'A packet of smokes and six cold cans of piss' (hence also 'hit the piss', 'sink some piss', or the British 'go on the piss', to go drinking) – making the link more literal, a newspaper ad encourages us to 'Get a Little John: the Travelling Urinal holds two bottles of beer'; 3. piss!, pish! – an exclamation of anger, frustration (the latter from 1592)

piss-ant – 1. (adjective) inconsequential, irrelevant, small, worthless; 2. (noun) a person possessing one of these qualities e.g. 'That little piss-ant keeps sticking his nose where it doesn't belong' (US use) (the word's original meaning is simply an ant, from the first element of 'pismire' (which in fact also means 'ant') plus, redundantly, 'ant'; 'pismire' – a fourteenth-century equivalent of the modern meaning of 'piss-ant': from 'pyss', urine (in reference to the acrid smell of an anthill) and 'mire', an ant (probably from Old Norse 'maurr', an ant, and perhaps distantly connected with the Greek 'myrmex' and the Latin 'formica'); the term is applied contemptuously to people from 1569 e.g. 'He is as angry as a pissemyre, /Though that he have al that he kan desire'(Chaucer, *The Summoner's Tale*, ll.1825–6)) piss around/about – 1. to mess about, to waste time, to dawdle; 2. to waste someone's time, to annoy someone

piss-arse – insignificant, worthless

piss-artist – 1. a habitual drunk (i.e. someone who gets 'pissed' – from 1975); 2. a contemptible time-waster, a foolish show-off (from the drunkard's characteristic blend of boastfulness and incompetence …)

piss away – to waste through carelessness or neglect, to squander e.g. 'Take my advice, son, don't piss away your marriage for the sake of a bit of fun.'

piss-ball around – to idle away time, to mess around

piss-burnt – stained or damaged with (or as with) urine

piss-cutter – someone or something excellent; a clever or crafty person (US)

piss easy – very easy

piss for shits and giggles – to waste one's time e.g. 'Let's get outa here. We're just pissin' for shits and giggles.' (US)

piss in someone's pocket – to ingratiate oneself with, be on very familiar terms with (Australian)

I wouldn't (cross the road to) piss in his ear if his brain was on fire – he's the lowest of the low, beneath contempt (see also page 130)

piss in the wind – 1. to do something ineffectually, without making any impression (cf. French, 'ça ne pisse pas loin'); 2. to (intend to) do something futile e.g. 'You're pissing in the wind if you think she's going to sleep with you.' (Engraved in the massive portico of a small Amsterdam square is the inscription: *Homo Sapiens Non Pissat In Ventum.*)

piss it – to complete a task easily, to win effortlessly

piss it up (against) the wall – to waste money, to spend money foolishly, usually on drink, drugs or gambling (presumably on the principle that you don't buy bad beer, just rent it) e.g. 'I can't believe I got paid last week and I've pissed it all up the wall!'

piss off – 1. to upset, annoy; 2. to go away – frequently as an imperative exclamation (from 1958, chiefly British)

piss on someone's bonfire/chips – to spoil someone's enjoyment, to ruin a good situation e.g. 'Don't piss on his chips just because he ruined your party; it was an accident and he's said sorry.'

piss on/all over someone – to thoroughly defeat, to trounce someone e.g. 'You should have seen Chelsea play on Saturday; they pissed all over Arsenal.'

piss oneself – 1. to laugh heartily; 2. to be terrified

pissed – angry (US); drunk, intoxicated (UK)

pissed as a coot/fart/newt/rat – very drunk

pissed off – angry, upset, or depressed (British use – but first attested just after World War II, as US slang)

pissed up – very drunk

pisser – 1. a penis; 2. a bloke, a fellow; 3. something extraordinary or very funny (from 'piss oneself laughing'); 4. an upset e.g. 'I can't believe what a pisser it was losing my job.'

piss-flaps – 1. the female genitals, particularly the labia; 2. an exclamation of annoyance

piss-head – a drunkard, habitual drinker

pisshole – 1. a lavatory; 2. an unpleasant, dirty place; 3. a hole made by urine

piss-house – a lavatory; a privy

pissing – an intensifier e.g. 'Where's my pissing car key got to?'

piss-poor – terrible, of low quality, as in the business one-liner 'The 5 Ps: Preparation Prevents Piss-Poor Performance'

piss-proud – 1. having an erection on awaking in the morning (as caused by a full bladder); 2. (in the seventeenth and eighteenth centuries) excessively arrogant

piss-take – a joke, a tease, a send-up (derived from the phrase 'take the piss')

piss-taker – a person who takes the piss

pisstivity – a state of mind, being cranky or upset (US use) e.g. 'Her boyfriend coming home late had her in a real state of pisstivity.'

piss-ugly etc. – very ugly; piss- is used widely as pure intensifier for other adjectives e.g. piss-easy

piss-up – 1. a drunken spree, party, or pub-crawl; 2. a mess-up, a bungled event

piss-wet – very wet, soaked

pissy – 1. irritable, short-tempered; 2. weak, feeble, inferior (often applied to drinks)

pissy queen – a fastidious gay male (related to 'prissy queen')

pissy-arsed – insignificant, inferior

take the piss (out of someone) – 1. to make fun of, to tease, to ridicule; 2. to take advantage of, to exploit e.g. 'Just because she likes babysitting, it doesn't mean you can dump the kids on her every time you go out. That's just taking the piss.' The phrase conjures up the act of deflating someone (who is too 'full of himself') as you deflate your bladder when urinating. Its subsequent history is debatable (see also page 74 for an alternative): for some, when the word 'piss' became classified as vulgar, the phrase was modified to 'taking the micturations', which was then shortened to 'taking the mickey'; for others, it spawned the Cockney corruption 'taking the mickey' (or mick), from the rhyming slang for piss, 'Mickey bliss' – which led in turn to 'take the Michael', and even the facetious 'extract the Michael' – and thence back to 'extract the urine', literally and metaphorically all but identical to 'take the piss' …

Regional Dialects

In Yorkshire generally, piss was called wash or old wash – in dialect wesh or owd wesh (from the Old English *waescean*, *wascan*, to wash); around Huddersfield it was weeting (sometimes pronounced weeatin – meaning wetting, from OE *waetan*, to moisten); around the North Yorkshire coast, Lancashire, Derbyshire and the western counties as far south as Shropshire, its name was lant (as in the stale urine used in wool-scouring, from OE and Old Norse *hland*, urine); in the south and west it was sig (old or 'aged' urine, also used for scouring – akin to the OE *sigan* or *sincan*, to sink or fall); in the middle of Wales there was *Lleisw*, and in the west, *Lleishu*; in Gaelic it was *fual* (from the Old Irish *fúal*, from the root *voag*, to be wet) or *graith*.

Other common expressions, some of which survive today, included:

lye (which means any strong alkaline solution, here as used for washing, from the OE [*leah*,] *leag* – related to the Latin *lavare*, to wash), or chamber-lye (a recipe of 1577 exploits its antiseptic qualities: 'Take chamber ly, and salte, and seethe them to gether, and wash the places where the skin is cut of[f]')

lee (possibly related to 'lew', lukewarm, from OE *hleow*)

wetting (OE *woet*, wet; *woetan*, to wet), or netting

old swill (from OE *swilian*, to wash)

old pot (Late OE *pott*)

scour (from Middle Dutch *scuren*, to polish or clean, and Old French *escurer* – both probably from the Low Latin *excurare*, to clean off, or literally take good care of: *ex* – out, and *curare* – care for)

slops (from OE *sloppe*, dung)

French

il ne se sent plus pisser – he thinks the sun shines out of his arse (lit. he no longer feels himself pissing)

ça pisse – it's pissing down

il pleut comme une vache qui pisse – it's pissing down (lit. it's raining like a pissing cow)

ça l'a pris comme une envie de pisser – he suddenly got an urge to do it (lit. it seized him like the desire to piss)

les principes, je leur pisse dessus! – I couldn't give a shit about principles! (lit. I piss on their principles)

c'est comme si on pissait dans un violon – it's like pissing in the wind (lit. it's as if one were pissing in a violin)

laisse pisser (le mérinos)! – forget it! let them get on with it! (lit. let them/the merino piss)

ça ne pisse pas loin – it's nothing to shout about, to write home about (lit. it doesn't piss far – cf. the English 'pissing in the wind', evoking the same image)

son nez pissait le sang – blood was gushing, pouring from his nose (lit. his nose was pissing blood) *le réservoir pissait l'eau* – water was pouring, gushing out of the tank (lit. the tank was pissing water)

un pisseur de copie – a writer, journalist etc. who churns out rubbish

un pisseur, une pisseuse – a weak-bladdered individual, someone who is always going for a pee

une pisseuse – a female (pejorative)

pisseux, pisseuse – wishy-washy, insipid (colour); tatty, scruffy (appearance) (lit. pissy); *une odeur pisseuse* – a smell of piss

la chaude-pisse/les chaudes-pisses – clap (gonorrhoea)

un pisse-froid – a wet blanket (lit. a cold-pisser; also an adjective)

un pisse-vinaigre – a wet blanket; a skinflint (lit. a vinegar-pisser) (cf. the eighteenth-century English use of 'vinegar-pisser' to mean miser, and 'to piss vinegar', to be miserly)

de la pisse de l'âne – cat's piss (i.e. weak/unpleasant drink; lit. donkey's piss)

un pissenlit – a dandelion (lit. a piss-in-the-bed – like the English 'pissabed' – apparently deriving from the plant's diuretic properties); *manger les pissenlits par la racine* – to be pushing up the daisies, be dead and buried (lit. to eat the dandelions by the roots)

and, quite unrelated:

une pissaladière (noun) – a Provençal pizza with onions, anchovy fillets, and black olives (from the Provençal *pissaladiera*, from *pissalat*, anchovy purée, from Latin *piscis*, fish), which you might like to accompany with piscola, a cocktail made of Pisco, a brandy distilled from grapes grown in the warm and sunny regions of Chile and Peru, first produced in the Pisco province of Peru in the sixteenth century, mixed with Coca-Cola.

German

es pisst schon wieder – it's pissing down again

sich bepissen – to piss oneself; but *wir haben uns vor Lachen fast in die Hosen gemacht* – we almost pissed ourselves laughing (lit. we almost did it in our trousers from laughing – the nature of the excretion remains vague)

verpissen – 1. to piss on e.g. *das Bett verpissen* – to wet the bed (though more common is the vaguer '*ins Bett machen*', to do it into the bed); 2. to leave (reflexive – originally to leave in order to go and piss) e.g. '*verpiss dich!*', piss off!

eine Pissnelke – a girl who disappoints certain male expectations and is considered a prude (highly derogatory – lit. a piss-carnation/pink)

etwas im Urin haben/spüren – to feel it in one's bones: to know something intuitively (lit. to have/feel something in one's urine)

eine Pinkelpause – a toilet break, convenience stop (lit. a piddle-break), on long car journeys or walks, for the travellers to relieve themselves e.g. '*der Bus hielt zu einer Pinkelpause*' (from *pinkeln*, to widdle, pee, piddle, perhaps from the East-Friesian *pinkel*, penis, or originally, tip, top, and now *Pinkel*, a spicy sausage of bacon and groats … – *pinkeln*

is also to drizzle, as opposed to the harder downpour of
pissen)

ein Pipimädchen – a bimbo (lit. a wee-wee-girl)

das Pipifax – nonsense (wee-wee here acting as an intensifier
of the modified *die Faxen*, foolery, mischief, nonsense)

Bier wegtragen – to piss (lit. to carry away beer)

Twelve

Literature

A pissing-post was a common term for a public urinal, which was a good place to stick posters and trade cards, so that a well-publicised enterprise was one 'whose business and good qualities you may find upon all the Pissing-posts in town' (Tom Brown, founding father of gutter journalism, 1699). However, urinals and urine have been subject rather than setting for some words more illustrious – even if, as Flaubert has it, 'Les livres ne se font pas comme les enfants, mais comme les pyramides [...] et ça ne sert à rien! et ça reste dans le désert! [...] Les chacals pissent au bas et les bourgeois montent dessus.' (Books are made not like children but like pyramids [...] and they're just as useless! and they stay in the desert! [...] Jackals piss at their foot and the bourgeois climb up on them.) (Letter to Ernest Feydeau, Nov./Dec. 1857)

James Joyce, *Ulysses*
(Paris, 1922)

The final forty pages of this Modernist epic, in the last hours of the single day that it recounts, take the form of an internal monologue by Molly Bloom. Sentences and punctuation are swept away in the fast-flowing river of her stream-of-consciousness (forty pages and one single full stop); and the rare moments that she leaves the bed where she waits for her husband, the book's latter-day Ulysses – exchanging it for the chamber pot, to attend to her menstrual needs and to urinate – only reinforce this fluidity, as well as the theme of herself as symbolic of the female 'stream' bringing renewal and regeneration of life; her urine flows as freely as her voice – and her voice speaks several times of urine:

> O no there was the face lotion I finished the last of yesterday that made my skin like new I told him over and over again get that made up in the same place and dont forget it God only knows whether he did after all I said to him Ill know by the bottle anyway if not I suppose Ill only have to wash in my piss like beeftea or chickensoup … that disgusting Cameron behind the meat market or that other wretch with the red head behind the tree where the statue of the fish used to be when I was passing pretending he was pissing standing out for me to see it with his babyclothes up to one side … after the Comerfords party oranges and lemonade to make you feel nice and watery I went into 1 of

them it was so biting cold I couldnt keep it when was that
93 the canal was frozen [both the Royal and Grand Canals
froze over in 1893] yes it was a few months after a pity a
couple of the Camerons werent there to see me squatting
in the mens place meadero [Spanish: 'urinal'] … O Lord it
was rotten cold too that winter when I was only about ten
was I yes … standing at the fire with the little bit of a short
shift I had up to heat myself I loved dancing about in it then
make a race back into bed Im sure that fellow opposite used
to be there the whole time watching with the lights out in
the summer and I in my skin hopping around I used to love
myself then stripped at the washstand dabbing and creaming
only when it came to the chamber performance I put out the
light … wheres the chamber gone easy Ive a holy horror of its
breaking under me after that old commode I wonder was I
too heavy sitting on his knee … I hope my breath was sweet
after those kissing comfits easy God I remember one time
I could scout ['squirt'] it out straight whistling like a man
almost easy O Lord how noisy I hope theyre bubbles on it
for a wad of money from some fellow Ill have to perfume it in
the morning dont forget … O Lord what a row youre making
… I like letting myself down after in the hole as far as I can
squeeze and pull the chain then to flush it nice cool pins and
needles … I better not make an alnight sitting on this affair
they ought to make chambers a natural size so that a woman
could sit on it properly he kneels down to do it … I wonder
why he wouldnt stay the night … he could easy have slept in
there on the sofa in the other room I suppose he was as shy as
a boy he being so young hardly 20 of me in the next room hed
have heard me on the chamber arrah what harm …

John Irving, *The Water-Method Man*
(Black Swan, London, 1986)

This is the story of a man battling with a urinary-tract infection
(and a sadistic French urologist and his prescriptions and his
waiting room), its unhealthy narrow windings mirroring those
of the plot: through the juggling of lovers' matutinal rituals
with frequent peeing; the rescue of a pee-soaked victim of
homophobic urinal abuse and of a self-destroying diabetic
who dreams of bedwetting; the memories of excruciating
peeing in front of a urologist father; the drugged absence of
memory of a urethrectomy, even the all-encompassing pain
and membership of the Brotherhood of the Order of the
Golden Prick that welcome him back into consciousness;
and the happy ending of the limitless promise of his new,
improved, virginal penis. Here is just a taster:

> Odd and painful peeing is not new to me.
> Seven times in the last five years, I have suffered this
> unnameable disorder. Once it was the clap, but that's another
> story. Usually, the apparatus is simply stuck together in the
> morning. A careful pinch sets things right, or almost right.
> Urinating is often a challenge, the sensations always new and
> surprising. Also, it's time-consuming – your day spent in
> anticipation of the next time you'll have to pee. Sex, typically,
> is unmentionable. Orgasm is truly climactic. Coming is a
> slow experience – the long, astonishing journey of a rough
> and oversized ballbearing. In the past I had given up the act

altogether. Which drives me to drink, which makes the pee burn: an unfriendly circle … I opened the door, then, holding Merrill around the waist, pointing his pecker down into the pee mug … Then I closed the door again and steered Merrill back toward the sink. Somewhere along the way, he began to pee. Biggie's sharp laugh must have touched some nervous part of him, for he twitched, loosening my thumb's grip on the stein's lid, and found himself clamped in the pee mug. Wrestling away, he peed all over my knee. I caught up with him at the foot of his bed, where he spun about, still peeing in a high arch, his face with a child's look of bewildered pain. I stiff-armed him over the footboard and he landed limp on the bed, peed a final burst straight up in the air, then threw up on his pillow. I set the pee mug down, washed off his face, turned his pillow over and covered him with a heavy puff, but he lay rigid in the bed with his eyes like fuses. I washed the pee off me and used the medicine dropper to take pee from the pee mug and plunk it into the different test tubes: red, green, blue, yellow. Then I realized that I didn't know where the color chart was. I didn't know what color the red was supposed to change to, or what color was dangerous for the blue to change to, and whether the green was supposed to stay clear or get cloudy, and what yellow was for. I'd only watched Merrill test himself, because he'd always come around in time to interpret the colors …

Then a second passed, which took two hours, and I woke up in the postoperative room – the recovery room …

'We'd like you to try to urinate now,' she said to me.

'I just went,' I said. But she rolled me over on my side and slid a green pan under me.

'Please just try,' she coaxed. She was awfully nice.

So I started to go, even though I was sure I had nothing to pee. When the pain came, it was like an awareness of someone else's pain in another room – or even more distant, in another hospital. It was quite a lot of pain; I felt sorry for the person enduring it; I was all through peeing before I realized that it was my pain, realized that the operation was over.

Nicholson Baker, *The Mezzanine* (Granta Books, Cambridge, 1986)

… I pivoted and stationed myself at a urinal. I was just on the point of relaxing into a state of urination when two things happened. Don Vanci swept into position two urinals over from me, and then, a moment later, Les Guster turned off his tap. In the sudden quiet you could hear a wide variety of sounds coming from the stalls: long, dejected, exhausted sighs; manipulations of toilet paper; newspapers folded and batted into place; and of course the utterly carefree noise of the main activity: mind-boggling pressurized spatterings followed by sudden urgent farts that sounded like air blown over the mouth of a beer bottle. The problem for me, a familiar problem, was that in this relative silence Don Vanci would hear the exact moment I began to urinate. More important, the fact that I had not yet begun to urinate was known to him as well. I had been standing at the urinal when he walked into the bathroom – I should be fully in progress by now. What was my problem? Was I so timid that

I was unable to take a simple piss two urinals down from another person? We stood there in the intermittent quiet, unforthcoming. Though we knew each other well, we said nothing. And then, just as I knew would happen, I heard Don Vanci begin to urinate forcefully.

... one night in the very busy bathroom of a movie theater at the end of the movie, I discovered the trick. When someone takes his position next to you, and you hear his nose breathing and you sense his proven ability to urinate time after time in public, and at the same time you feel your own muscles closing on themselves as hermit crabs pull into their shells, imagine your self turning and dispassionately urinating onto the side of his head. Imagine your voluminous stream making fleeting parts in his hair, like the parts that appear in the grass of a lawn when you try to water it with a too-pressurized nozzle-setting. Imagine drawing an X over his face; watch him fending the spray off with his arm, puffing and spluttering to keep it from getting in his mouth; and his protestations: 'Excuse me? What are you doing? Hey!'

Geoffrey Chaucer, *The Canterbury Tales*

Chaucer included frequent pissing episodes in his epic collection of moral tales. The Wife of Bath says that she would hide nothing from her confidante – she'd reveal all, whether her husband committed a piddling offence like peeing against a wall, or a capital crime:

To hire biwreyed I my conseil al.
For hadde myn housbonde pissed on a wal,
Or doon a thyng that sholde han cost his lyf,
To hire ...
I wolde han toold his conseil every deel.

(*The Wife of Bath's Prologue*, ll.533–8)

A man sits by the fire reading of how wicked and hence how wretched mankind is; of how destructive womankind is; one of Socrates' wives gets so pissed off by his solemnity that she pisses on his head – to which his only response is to remain an infuriating model of stoicism:

No thyng forgat he the care and the wo
That Socrates hadde with his wyves two;
How Xantippa caste pisse upon his heed.
This sely man sat stille as he were deed.

(*The Wife of Bath's Prologue*, ll.727–30)

William Shakespeare

Even in the horror story of *Macbeth*, Shakespeare lets lavatorial humour creep in:

Porter: Drink, sir, is a great provoker of three things.
Macduff: What three things does drink especially provoke?
Porter: Marry, sir, nose-painting, sleep, and urine. Lechery,

sir, it provokes, and unprovokes; it provokes the desire, but takes away the performance. (II, iii)

Two carriers complain about their lodgings in *Henry IV Part I*:

Why, they will allow us ne'er a jordan; and then we leak in your chimney; and your chamber-lye breeds fleas like a loach'. (Second Carrier; II, ii)

French Literature

François Rabelais, *Five books of the lives, heroic deeds and sayings of Gargantua and his son Pantagruel* (translated into English by Sir Thomas Urquhart of Cromarty and Peter Antony Motteux). These books, published in the mid-sixteenth century, describe the adventures of two giants, a father, Gargantua, and his son, Pantagruel; they are extravagantly satirical, and bursting with bodily discharges.

Chapter 1.XI.: Of the youthful age of Gargantua.
  Gargantua … pissed in his shoes, shit in his shirt, and wiped his nose on his sleeve – he did let his snot and snivel fall in his pottage, and dabbled, paddled, and slobbered everywhere.

Chapter I.XVII.: How Gargantua paid his welcome to the Parisians, and how he took away the great bells of Our Lady's Church.

... I will now give them their wine, but it shall be only in sport. Then smiling, he untied his fair braguette, and drawing out his mentul into the open air, he so bitterly all-to-bepissed them, that he drowned two hundred and sixty thousand, four hundred and eighteen, besides the women and little children. Some, nevertheless, of the company escaped this piss-flood by mere speed of foot, who, when they were at the higher end of the university, sweating, coughing, spitting, and out of breath, they began to swear and curse, some in good hot earnest, and others in jest.

Chapter I.XXXVI.: How Gargantua demolished the castle at the ford of Vede, and how they passed the ford.

... In the meantime his mare pissed to ease her belly, but it was in such abundance that it did overflow the country seven leagues, and all the piss of that urinal flood ran glib away towards the ford of Vede, wherewith the water was so swollen that all the forces the enemy had there were with great horror drowned, except some who had taken the way on the left hand towards the hills.

Gabriel Chevallier's *Clochemerle* was described by the *Times Literary Supplement* as 'a full-blooded uproarious farce in the Rabelaisian tradition,' the 'classic comic novel of provincial France'. *Clochemerle* describes in languorous and absurd detail the 1920s political shenanigans in the sleepy little town of Clochemerle-en-Beaujolais, where much wonderful wine is

produced and consumed, and where the men all lust after the
few attractive women.

The story opens with a conversation between the
Machiavellian mayor, M. Piéchut, and the schoolmaster,
Tafardel, 'the quality of whose breath made him a formidable
opponent at close quarters'.

> The mayor was a clever fellow ... Whenever he wanted to
> have a serious conversation with the schoolmaster, he would
> take him for a walk. By this means, he always got him in
> profile.
>
> 'We must think of something, Tafardel, which will be a
> shining example of the supremacy of a progressive town
> council.'
>
> 'I entirely agree with you, Monsieur Piéchut. But I must
> point out that there is already the war memorial.' ...
>
> 'I want to build a urinal, Tafardel.'
>
> 'A urinal?' the schoolmaster cried out, startled and
> impressed. The matter, he saw at once, was obviously of
> extreme importance.
>
> 'Yes, a public convenience,' said the mayor.
>
> Now when a matter of such consequence is revealed to you
> suddenly and without warning, you cannot produce a ready-
> made opinion regarding it. And at Clochemerle, precipitancy
> detracts from the value of a judgement ...

The urinal is duly built – opposite the church – and arouses
endless controversy. Even the curé speaks out:

'... we Christians of Clochemerle, shall not shrink from the task of driving out all those who have brought impurity to the very doors of our beloved church. On this monument of infamy ... let us wield the pickax of deliverance! My brethren, my dear brethren, our watchword shall be – demolition!'

The political complications go from bad to worse; troops are sent in; and finally the urinal is dynamited.

In Samuel Beckett's *En attendant Godot* (*Waiting for Godot*), most famously known as a play in which 'nothing happens, twice', the defiantly undramatic nature of Beckett's Absurdist drama is underlined by the merging of actors and audience. They, as much as we, are waiting for something to happen, for the all-important Godot to make an entrance – and if we find ourselves getting bored, wondering instead when the interval will arrive, we are in good company. After a typical exchange of platitudes Vladimir excuses himself, asking Estragon to save his place. Estragon tells him where he should go, and tells him when he gets back that he's missed some wonderful stuff – though we know better; the only drama has been the missing actor's own peeing ...

German Literature

Günter Grass, *Die Blechtrommel*
(*The Tin Drum*)
(tr. Ralph Manheim, Martin Secker & Warburg, 1962)

In the first volume of Grass's great Danzig Trilogy, the dwarfish and hunchbacked Oskar, having stopped growing at age three and honed his drumming skills in personal and political battles, joins a band that plays at a pub which sells onions to those who've forgotten how to cry. With his drum alone, he reduces the clients to snivelling children bathed in memories – and then makes them not only cry, but piss their pants, communally and gloriously uncontrollably. (The passage is not just farcically brilliant, but a vivid satire on the post-war generation's readiness for a false remembrance intended only to exonerate, not to illuminate, in a comfortably 'collective' guilt, everyone's and therefore no one's).

Without any notion of what I was going to do, I made myself understood … It was a three-year-old Oskar who picked up those drumsticks. I drummed my way back, I drummed up the world as a three-year-old sees it. And the first thing I did to these postwar humans incapable of a real orgy was to put a harness on them: … they took each other by the hands,

turned their toes in, and waited for me, their Pied Piper. ...
When I had registered my success – childlike merriment on
every hand – I decided to scare them out of their wits ... so
obtaining the results for which Schmuh required onions; the
ladies and gentlemen wept great round, childlike tears, the

ladies and gentlemen were scared pink and green; their teeth
chattered, they begged me to have mercy. And so, to comfort
them, and in part to help them back into their outer and
undergarments, their silks and satins, I drummed ... Then,
at last, wishing to give all those present, including Schmuh

the head man, something by which to remember their day in kindergarten, I gave them all permission to do number one [*ein kleines Geschäftchen* – lit. a little business] … I said on my drum: now, children, you may go [*nun dürft ihr Kinderchen*]. And they availed themselves of the opportunity. All the ladies and gentlemen, Schmuh the host, even the far-off washroom attendant, all the little children wet themselves, psss, psss they went [*pißpißpiß machten sie, näßten alle die Höschen*], they all crouched down and listened to the sound they were making and they all wet their pants.

Latin Literature

Catullus, the bitchy poetry critic, suggested that the *Annals* of Volusius would make better loo-paper than poetry ('*Annales Volusi, cacata charta.*')

In Catullus's own *Poem 39*, Egnatius – his rival in love (for the promiscuous Clodia) – constantly smiles, showing unnaturally white teeth. Catullus suggests (in lines 18–21) this is because people in Spain have unusual toothpaste:

> quod quisque minxit, hoc sibi solet mane
> dentem atque russam defricare gingivam
> ut, quo ista vester expolitior dens est
> hoc te amplius bibisse praedicet loti.

This may be translated as, 'What each person pees, he regularly rubs on his teeth and red gums in the morning; so the shinier your teeth are, the more of your piss you must have drunk!'

Thirteen

Music

There are many urinary band names, including Piss Ant, Chriss Piss, Piss Factory, Adolf and the Piss Artists, Piss Happy, Children Piss on Authority, No Place to Piss, Anal Piss-Machine, Piss On Authority, Urine Junkies, and songs with such evocative titles as *A Piss in the Ocean* and *I Wouldn't Piss In Your Ear If Your Brain Was On Fire*.

Many songs make explicit mention of piss. They might talk of pissing in the wind (Badly Drawn Boy, *Pissing in the Wind*; Neil Young, *Ambulance Blues*), in a river (Patti Smith, *Pissing in a River*), or up a rope (Ween, *Piss up a Rope*); they might throw in a line about what it's like pissing on oneself (Jane's Addiction, *Standing in the Shower … Thinking*), or 'how it hurts when I pee' (Nirvana, *Mexican Seafood*).

Some are all about pee. The Australian alternative band Regurgitator's *I Piss Alone* relates a schoolboy's existential agony at the sense of inadequacy the communal urinal brings: the quiet, the sound of fear, the 'pressure of the other boys' that he can't match; the longing for solitude, for a place with a lock on the door so he can stop and let it flow, for a 'world where pissing troughs are obsolete'.

Frank Zappa's *Why Does it Hurt When I Pee? (Joe's Garage)* tells the story of Joe, who, shortly after his liaison with the taco stand lady, makes the terrible discovery that it hurts when he pees – and he deduces that he got it from the toilet seat, that 'it' jumped up and grabbed him, that since his balls feel like a pair of maracas he's probably caught the 'Gon-o-ka-ka-khackus': 'Ai-ee-ai-ee-ahhhh!'

With equivalent histrionics, the Cookie Makin Satan Haters, in *I Slit My Wrist While Takin a Piss*, tell in all its grisly

detail the tale of how, after a few beers, a fly zip can become an agent of agony: a lovely, long relieving pee – then, zipping up, the sudden pain, hand through a window pane in shock, blood and torn pubic hair … But there's a happy ending: the vital organs are preserved intact. Nothing else matters, only that he's got his sack back.

Chumbawumba's Nineties anthem *Tubthumping* deals, less theatrically, with the simple cause and effect of drinking and peeing (the drinking of a whisky drink, a vodka drink, a lager drink, a cider drink …), neatly linked in the oft-repeated time-wasting idiom of 'pissing the night away'.

Similarly, Jerry Jeff Walker's *Pissin' in the Wind* evokes a life of waste, of making the same mistakes over and over, through the image of pissing in the wind, it blowing on your friends, and that being all you'll have to tell your grandchildren: in the end it's all just pissing in the wind, pissing in the sink.

In the slightly surreal metaphors of *No Shit (Give Piss a Chance)*, Henry Fiat's Open Sore asks his sweetheart what's better for her – 'number one or number two, a pint of piss or a plate of poop' – all secret code for: him or me – 'shit from him or piss from me'; he amorously begs his baby to 'take no shit' from the other guy, and, rather, to give piss a chance.

Continuing in the romantic vein, Dog Fashion Disco's *Pour Some Urine on Me* is a colourful ode to 'urine love', asking the angelic addressee to open the floodgates, to 'rain down on me'; to embalm the scenery with golden showers and acid rain, to make 'pee-pee and poetry'. The horror punk/glam metal band Murderdolls' *Love at First Fright* is the touching description of how the singer knew it was true love just when he 'saw you piss on the rug' – heart fluttering, you're the only one for me; while the lustful ideal of NOFX's *See Her Pee* is in seeing a gorgeous girl in action – and not just anywhere, but between parked cars, on a well-lit street.

By contrast, Green Day's *Platypus (I Hate You)* is a jolly song of pure hate that ends with the unambiguous dream of 'you' going down head first into the ground, and the singer standing up above, 'just to piss on your grave'.

More principled hatred is the subject of The Coup's *Piss on your Grave*, one of the numerous politically angled pissing songs. It is addressed to the late George Washington, 'down in hell', by a singer standing on his grave. He's taking a guided tour of the Arlington National Cemetery, and is incorporated into the tour guide's patter as 'the gentleman with the afro', standing on 'the grave of America's first and greatest hero' – and, unbeknownst to him, about to piss on it. The song ends with the glory of unzipping, piss hitting the ground, the sigh of relief, the clicking of the other tourists' cameras – G.W. made to pay for his sins, for all the steaks he ate while others starved.

Tom Paxton's *We're Filling a Bottle for Ronnie* has a different presidential target. It recounts the Reagan's first strike in a 'war on drugs' with urine as the weapon:

I go to my job every morning. I go to my job every day.
My buddies and me we're all plumbers and we can't
complain, for the job is okay.
So there we are drinking our coffee and smoking a last
cigarette,
When in comes the foreman all red in the face, saying, "This
is the hottest one yet."
So Louie says, "What's the big problem,
What's got your dander up, Joe?"
Joe, he goes, "Look in the paper my friend,
It's there for the whole world to know.
The President's gonna stop all these drugs,
by testing us one at a time."
So all of us lays down our tools on the floor.
And we busily start fighting crime.

Chorus:

We're filling a bottle for Ronnie, we're filling it up to the
brim,
And we'll never rest till we all pass the test, for we all think
the world of him.
We're filling a bottle for Ronnie, and we'll never kick up a
fuss,
For we're only doing to that little bottle what Ronnie's been
doing to us.

The people who work in the White House,
According to what I read here,
Are gonna be filling their own little bottles

To make sure the message is clear.
At Cabinet meeting with Ronnie,
They're gonna be taking a break,
They'll call a recess at the Gipper's request,
And they'll all have some wee-wee to make.

[Chorus]

They're gonna be testing our children,
And you can be certain of that.
They're gonna be testing our old maiden aunts
And they're gonna be testing our cats.
They used to go looking for traitors
Who commonly hid under beds,
Now, 'stead of them stirrin' up all of this urine,
They ought to try testing their heads!

Similarly, Mojo Nixon and Skid Roper protest against compulsory urine testing in *I Ain't Gonna Piss in no Jar*. They ask why everyone is so scared of drugs, and declare that they won't 'pee pee in no cup unless Nancy Reagan's gonna drink it up'; they dream of retaliation, of the poetic justice of surrounding the White House with a moat of stinking, steaming, yellow urine which Ronald and Nancy would have to navigate in a boat; they invoke the angry spirit of Thomas Jefferson from beyond the grave; and, in defiant conclusion, they'll sooner be thrown in jail, be skewered with hot pokers, than part with a drop of 'peepee' against their will.

Michael Collins's *The Jar Song* has very nearly the same refrain, variations on the theme of 'you ain't gonna get me to piss in no jar' – this time in the context both of professional life and of politics. He will submit to the typing test, give personal references, reveal personal preferences – but will not piss in a jar. And in the States you can't be a political star either, he says, without being ready to fill a carafe; he mocks the land of the brave and the free as being more like the home of the KGB – though 'not even in the USSR can they get anybody to piss in a jar.'

Urinetown: The Musical on Broadway depicts a future, rather than a present, urinary dystopia. The *Seattle Times* critic Misha Berson characterizes it as 'Simpsons and South Park meet Weill and Brecht'.

> Set in a Gotham-like city overwrought by ecological disaster, Urinetown is a tale of greed, corruption, love, and revolution in a time when water is worth its very weight in gold. A depletion of the earth's water supply has led to a government-enforced ban on private toilets. The privilege to pee is regulated by a single, malevolent corporation, which profits by charging admission for one of mankind's most basic needs. (BroadwayWorld.com)

The opening number is a rousing welcome to Urinetown, a town of a single restroom, unisex by design. The song addresses the audience who 'have come to see what it's like when people can't pee free' – warning that the first act lasts an hour so it might be prudent to 'go now', for there's often a queue. (This recalls the self-referentiality to Beckett's *Waiting for Godot* (see page p. 126), only here peeing is the drama rather than the lack of it; the act of going for a piss is shifted from the actors, as part of an absence of activity which might reduce the audience to idly pondering the state of their own bladders, to the audience who should be eager not to miss a moment of the urinary action.)

Making musical pissing into real-life lyrics is the famous Rolling Stones 'We piss anywhere, maaan ...' anecdote. On 12 March 1965 'The Last Time' topped the British charts and was released in the States, where it got to number eight. Six days later, on their way back to London after a gig in Romford, the Stones' Bill Wyman needed a pee, and the band stopped in their Daimler at the Romford Road petrol station. But for some reason the station mechanic, Charles Keeley, refused to open the facilities, and told the band to leave. The Stones are said to have sung 'We will piss anywhere man' as Bill Wyman, Mick Jagger, and Brian Jones urinated on the garage wall. Two days later the *Daily Express* reported the incident and the police began investigating; the Stones were fined five pounds. But more significant than the cash was the cachet – in styling themselves as the bad-boys, in contrast to the squeaky clean Beatles, this flamboyant pissing in the Sixties was as powerful as what American record-label boss Gary 'Pig' Gold calls their 'jet-setting, trend-setting string of designer drug busts of the Seventies'.

Fourteen

Piss-artists

Film

Lavatories are rarely seen on television, but films seem positively to revel in excretion. The fashion may have been started in 1960 by Alfred Hitchcock, who was enthusiastic about lavatories, put one shockingly into *Psycho* (which caused more of a stir at the time than the shower scene), and once said the length of a film should be in inverse proportion to the endurance of the human bladder.

At the beginning of *Never Say Never Again* (1983), Sean Connery, as James Bond, is sent to a health farm to get rid of dangerous free radicals. From across the examination room a nurse says, 'Mr. Bond, I need a urine sample. If you could fill this beaker for me?' He replies, 'From here?'

Buddies Jim Carrey and Jeff Daniels share a gross urinary scene in *Dumb and Dumber* (1994). Jeff is driving at high speed along the highway in a ridiculous truck when Jim, in the passenger seat, gets desperate to pee and relieves himself noisily into several empty beer bottles. As he finishes they are stopped by a policeman, who sees the bottles, accuses them of drinking, and starts to drink one himself ...

My Favourite Year (1982) features Peter O'Toole as a womaniser, who goes into the Ladies' in a TV studio. An old woman says primly, 'This is for ladies only!' He replies, 'So is this, madam, but every now and then I have to run water through it.'

The heroine of the French short film *La Pisseuse* (1997) is looking forward to the day ahead – but among the events that conspires to make her miss her oral exam is a growing need to pee that she cannot satisfy ... (English title: *Missy Pissy*).

The tagline of another short, *Pissed* (2000), is 'Two women ... one bathroom stall ... zero couth. Welcome to the ladies room'. On the other hand, the US comedy (ultra-) short *Pee Shy* (2000) speaks, for its four full minutes, straight to the heart of any man who has ever used a public urinal: 'With a little plastic divider, and a lot of love, we can beat this thing!'

The Lion in Winter (1968) stars Katherine Hepburn as Queen Eleanor of Acquitaine, in a love-hate relationship with her husband King Henry II (Peter O'Toole). He wants to name the spotty exploitative brat who is his youngest son John (Nigel Terry) as his heir, while she schemes in favour of Richard (Anthony Hopkins). One choice exchange is between the regal rivals:

> JOHN: Poor John. Who says poor John? Don't everybody sob at once! My God, if I went up in flames there's not a living soul who'd pee on me to put the fire out!
> RICHARD: Let's strike a flint and see.

In *The Aviator* (2004), Howard Hughes (Leonardo DiCaprio) slides, via the twin traumas of love and money, and by way of art and plane crashes, into obsessive insanity. Shutting himself into his screening room, he recites his compulsive mantras and longs for cleanliness – while sinking into slovenliness. He survives on milk alone, and uses the bottles to pee into. A striking panning camera shot unfolds upon a long row of bottles, all filled with yellowish liquid of different amounts and shades, like the tally of days scratched into the wall of a prison cell.

Interactive

Nintendo's *Conker's Bad Fur Day* (for the N64 console) stars Conker the hungover party animal, tossed in his morning-after misery from one themed world to the next, and is squarely aimed at the student market, with an infamous sequence in which Conker drinks himself silly and we share the wondrous joys that come only from peeing on strangers. Critics praise the physics and design of the revolutionary pee stream technology, from the curvature of the arc to the staining and the dripping.

In Sony's *Dog's Life* (for Play Station 2), you are Jake, the loveable mutt on a mission to rescue the dog-napped Daisy, traversing the USA and doing all that a dog does: sniffing out food, playing fetch, chasing cats and chickens, and marking your territory – for Jake can fart, poo and pee. You can also switch from a third-person perspective to 'Smell-o-vision', a first-person canine view of the world in which all is sepia except the brightly-coloured smells.

Visual

While the first meeting of piss and visual art may have been the prosaic practice of artists washing their canvases in urine, or early photographers their plates, the relationship has come a long way since then. Andy Warhol's *Oxidation Paintings*, produced in the 1970s, are tawny iridescent blotches made of copper paint smeared on canvas and peed on, blooming into colour as the uric acid of the urine oxidized the metal in the copper base and caused it to discolour in patterns determined by the movement of the 'painter'.

Warhol reported to Bob Colacello (journalist, and editor of Warhol's magazine *Interview*) that his 'Piss Paintings' were a 'parody of Jackson Pollock – referring to rumours that Pollock would urinate on a canvas before delivering it to a dealer or client he didn't like' – and referring also to Pollock's technique of dripping paint on to flat canvas, invoking the idea of painting as a metaphor for pissing.

Pollock is also reported as having been assailed, when he stood back and looked at one of the first of his own drip paintings, by a memory of 'himself standing beside his father on a flat rock, watching his father pissing, making patterns on the surface of the stone … and he wanted to do the same thing when he grew up' – the waters of the bladder clearly run deep. More famously, Pollock, irritated that a mural of his had been cropped in order to fit on to Peggy Guggenheim's wall, peed into a fireplace at a party, in front of his patron and her friends. Indeed, so tireless was he in his public urinations (reportedly all stemming from pissing competitions he had with his brother as a boy) that he earned the sobriquet 'Jack the Dripper' and was rumoured to have 'dripped' even on Guggenheim's bed. The fact that he called five of his paintings *Number 1* might hence be interpreted as a subtle blend of toilet humour and a yearning for an originary art unsullied by any precedent.

Freud, in his *Civilization and Its Discontents*, imagines the dawn of civilisation as a scene of urination: 'Psycho-analytic material, incomplete as it is and not susceptible to clear interpretation, nevertheless admits of a conjecture – a fantastic-sounding one – about the origin of this human feat. It is as though primal man had the habit, when he came in contact with fire, of satisfying an infantile desire connected with it, by putting it out with a stream of urine. Putting out fire by micturating was therefore a kind of sexual act with a male, and enjoyment of sexual potency in homosexual competition. The first person to renounce this desire and spare the fire was able to carry it off with him and subdue it to his own use. By damping down the fire of his own sexual excitation, he had tamed the natural force of fire. This great cultural conquest was thus the reward for his renunciation of instinct.'

Warhol's *Oxidation* Series and Pollock's drip paintings, along with the works of Mapplethorpe and Serrano (see below) choose primordial instinct (pissing) over all the (self-) control of civilization and of art, enacting a return to the dawn of man – or just to infancy. Warhol parodying Pollock can, similarly, be seen as choosing the games of the gay over the responsibilities of the straight: displaying 'sexual potency in homosexual competition' rather than sensibly saving the fire, for the woman to tend; for Freud, it was 'as though woman had been appointed guardian of the fire which was held captive on the domestic hearth, because her anatomy made it impossible for her to yield to the temptation of this desire' to pee – at least so comfortably, efficiently – or flamboyantly. To be the better pisser is to be the better painter. Thus the connection of painting and pissing leads us from public bed-wetting to the origins of civilisation and the nature of art.

Meanwhile, back in 1917 Marcel Duchamp presented a 'Fountain' – an off-the-shelf urinal – for display at a New York exhibition, by the pseudonymic R. Mutt, whose signature adorns the urinal. It was rejected, and is known to us only in photographs, in a copy made by the artist in the Fifties, and in the floods of commentary that have streamed into and out of it. This supine (half 'inverted' – this was a euphemism of the time for being homosexual; and urinals were common sites of gay pickups) urinal overturns the boundaries between art and non-art, public and private behaviour – and hence also Freud's concept of 'civilisation'.

This man-made female object for exclusively male functions is confusing in all sorts of ways. How can a piece of plumbing, designed to receive male liquid, be a fountain that spouts water? If the name, the Fountain, is a reference to the penis, what about the object, the rounded compact shape that suggests the female anatomy, made to contain its own fluids? As an existent object, too, it causes difficulties; the form in which people got to see the Fountain after its ignominious ejection from the 'open exhibition' was as a photograph taken by Alfred Stieglitz – the object itself later disappeared, as did almost all of Duchamp's 'original ready-mades' – which has been examined for its numerous oddities. These include the strange light and shadow, and the peculiar reflections, reminiscent of pooling urine, in the urinal's upper lip – such pooling seems to go against the laws of gravity and of perspective: to make visual sense of it as urine, we have to imagine the urinal properly installed on a wall and ourselves hovering around the ceiling gazing down upon the urinary lake.

While the urinal itself has been taken as sexist exclusion of the female (the stand-up pissoir once common on French streets was a 'convenience' only for the male public), peoples as early as the Greeks had made fountains that played similar games with the sex of urinators. A second-century Hellenistic Fountain Nymph has a strong, horizontal flow of water, projected out of a round vaginal channel that passes through the pelvis of the marble standing female, and into a basin which it fills and overflows from. And adapting replicas of classical statues to modern household fixtures was quite common: the Venus de Milo became in 1896 the Vénus de Mille-eaux – reduced to a surface for pasted-on adverts for prosaically fashionable watering places.

Warhol had willing partners in piss. Colacello describes how 'Andy paid Victor [Hugo] to be the collaborator. He would come to the Factory to urinate on canvases that had already been primed with copper-based paint by Andy or Ronnie Cutrone, who was a second ghost pisser, much appreciated by Andy' – and given practical instruction by Warhol himself, as he notes in his diary: 'I told Ronnie not to pee when he gets up in the morning, to try to hold it until he gets to the office, because he takes lots of vitamin B so the canvas turns a really pretty color when it's his pee.' Warhol reportedly peed on the first few of his paintings, and was then happy to delegate to the steady stream of 'boys who'd come to lunch and drink too much wine, and find it funny or even flattering to be asked to help Andy 'paint.'' He was said even to have fed them a particular brand of Mexican beer because he liked its effect. And since urine is as rich in DNA as blood, the paintings became (self-)portraits of every one of their piss-painters (as well as a record of their drinking habits), like territories marked, identities cryptically traced.

One unchoreographed contribution was made by the British producer Brian Eno, the creator of ambient music, with a reputation for intellectual curiosity and experimentation, but also for a bizarre sense of humour. In his diary of the year 1995, *A Year With Swollen Appendices* (1996), he relates his chagrin at discovering the Fountain on display at the New York Museum of Modern Art, being treated like a holy relic, where its message, he felt, was that 'I can call any old urinal – or anything else for that matter – a piece of art'.

More pressingly, though, he continues:

I've always wanted to urinate on that piece of art, to leave my small mark on art history. I thought this might be my last chance – for each time it was shown it was more heavily defended. At MoMa it was being shown behind glass, in a large display case. There was, however, a narrow slit between the two front sheets of glass. It was about three-sixteenths of an inch wide.

I went to the plumber's on the corner and obtained a couple of feet of clear plastic tubing of that thickness, along with a similar length of galvanized wire. Back in my hotel room, I inserted the wire down the tubing to stiffen it. Then I urinated into the sink and, using the tube as a pipette, managed to fill it with urine. I then inserted the whole apparatus down my trouser-leg and returned to the museum, keeping my thumb over the top end so as to ensure that the urine stayed in the tube.

At the museum, I positioned myself before the display case, concentrating intensely on its contents. There was a guard standing behind me and about 12 feet away. I opened my fly and slipped out the tube, feeding it carefully through the slot in the glass. It was a perfect fit, and slid in quite easily until its end was poised above the famous john. I released my thumb, and a small but distinct trickle of my urine splashed on to the work of art.

Whether as an act of derangement, a childish prank, or an astute artistic statement, Duchamp would probably have loved it.

A link has also been made between Warhol and Mapplethorpe: Colacello claims that the idea for the piss-paintings came from New York sex clubs and gay bath houses, including one called the Toilet, where 'there were tubs and troughs where naked men lay for other naked men to urinate on them' – 'It was like a Robert Mapplethorpe photograph come alive.' Others have noted the example of Pasolini's 1968 film *Teorema*, in which Terence Stamp plays a man who becomes an artist and urinates on a canvas in his search for the ultimate aesthetic methodology.

Charles Demuth, a good friend of Marcel Duchamp, and strongly influenced by him, added his drop to the ocean of urine art with *Three Sailors Urinating* (1930), in which urine is aimed in the general direction of the viewer, and *Two Men Urinating*, in which the beholder is actually where the urinal should be. So Demuth reduced audience to urinal even as Duchamp elevated urinal to artwork. These erotic watercolours were not, however, meant for public consumption – so the 'viewer' is only the artist himself, his close friends, and those meant to find the works after his death; thus they feel like intimate confessions or long-buried memoirs. But where Mapplethorpe's triptych *Jim and Tom, Sausalito* (1977), which shows in each of its panels Jim pissing into Tom's eager mouth, in raking light and ominous shadow, creates a sense of evil that engages our moral judgement, Demuth's watercolour sailors seem sweet, even innocent – as if exempted from the unhappiness of Freud's 'civilisation', posing more challenging questions of what is sexually permissible, or clean and dirty.

One of the most controversial pieces of piss was Andres Serrano's *Piss Christ* (1989), which depicts Christ on the cross submerged in a vat of the artist's own urine, one of a series of various religious and cultural icons immersed in various bodily fluids, dramatically closing the gap between the divine and the corporeal.

More prettily piss-related are the *Piss Flowers* of Helen Chadwick (1991) – she and her husband peed into mounds of snow (her piss strong and warm, his diffuse and cooler), and cast the cavities in bronze to make 'flowers', great white blooms on a green carpet, which she saw as being erotic as a result of their source in sensual bodily collaboration.

Ashley Bickerton's *Joan* (1995) is a satirical portrait of an upper-class New York woman (the artist's main clientele) ingloriously crouching and pissing; while Richard Hamilton's *Esquisse* (1972) preserves the discreet nature of a woman in the same position, a lithograph capturing something elusive as a covertly taken photo does.

And the piss needn't be static. Annie Sprinkle, as a performing Post-Porn Modernist (1989), urinates on stage to blur boundaries of public and private activity; and Paul Quinn's *Pissing Thing* (1992) is a grotesque little sculpture whose only point is to perpetually piss, making peeing into a self-sufficient act, both mechanical and aesthetic.

Gilbert and George's *Friendship pissing* (1989) and *Urinight* (1987) show men pissing together; in the former the streams of urine – depicted as crossing; this is all about fraternity, the sharing of a specifically male activity (as were Demuth's *Sailors*, holding one another's penises – though these were about eroticism as much as comradeship); Pierre et Gilles' *Le Petit Jardinier* (1993), meanwhile, stresses at once the erotic and the pleasurable nature of pissing, as enacted in a flower garden; Larry Clark's *Images* from the film *Kids* (1995) are photographs of a boy pissing while another sits in the bath next to him – erotic because they are so frank, and because the boys are so oblivious to the eroticism. Tony Tasset's *I peed in my pants* (1994) makes the embarrassing into the assertive and self-possessed, the accidental into the active, in a self-portrait of him standing with arms folded, as he calmly pisses himself.

Internet inventors suggest a helping hand for those artistically or biologically challenged: Pee-in-a-can (a salty yellow less-than-lemonade), for the wintertime fun of writing your name – or creating an artwork – in the snow. The advantage of avoiding exposure might seem a disadvantage to some brash and brave souls – for them, there's the larger-than-life penis-shaped can for boasting without the goose bumps; this might appeal less to women, though. Having dreamed up a self-heating coffee-can, the geeks take the logical next step, and have pee emerge steaming in the frosty air, for added efficacy and poetic realism; or, instead of an expensive heating element, they suggest, a flexible bladder could be linked to the can with a tube long enough to keep the 'pee' warm next to the skin, beneath one's thick winter coat.

Brussels Spout

A little pissing boy, the *Manneken Pis*, fills a niche on a Brussels
street corner close to the Grand Place, pissing calmly away all
day and every day. He was born in the late fourteenth century
and seems originally to have been known as Little Julian; but
he was lost, or just grew tatty, and was replaced in 1619 by a
brother in bronze. There are various legends about his origins:
he was created in honour of a boy who used his pee to douse
an arsonist's flame and save the town from destruction; a boy
peed against the door of a witch who lived where the fountain
now stands, enraging her so much that she turned him into a
statue cursed to pee for eternity; a father lost his children and
finally found his son peeing in this spot, and in his relief and
gratitude had a statue constructed in commemoration; the son
of a duke was caught peeing against a tree in the midst of battle
and was immortalised thus as a symbol of the nation's military
courage. Others prefer to see him simply as a kid who's taking
a pee.

He has become something of a national symbol (though
what exactly he means to his countrymen is not quite clear
– cheeky defiance, plucky survival …?); certainly life has not
been dull for him. He was given his first costume in 1698
by a rich governor, another by Louis XV in apology for
his kidnapping by French soldiers; and has since amassed
a wardrobe of five or six hundred outfits from visiting
dignitaries; he normally gets dressed up around his birthday.
He has also been stolen by plundering soldiers – and by the

jealous citizens of a city in Flanders, who lay competitive claim to the country's oldest pissing-boy statue. Perched as he is, high up on his pedestal, his size always takes people by surprise – he is a diminutive 55.5cm tall; but that hasn't stopped them from making him smaller still, in a million replicas for sale, among the most popular being shiny brass corkscrews, in which the penis and its curling flow of golden liquid have become the worm – all accurately portraying him as left-handed. He has lately acquired a sister, *Jeanneke Pis*, created by local merchants in the 1980s in response to the Manneken's popularity. She squats to pee, with a half-thoughtful, half-mischievous smile on her face, but she lives in a side alley and is in comparison sadly neglected. An impassively pissing boy must somehow say something to people that a squatting girl just can't.

Fifteen

Family Pets ...

Cats

Some experts claim that cats can be taught to use an ordinary human lavatory. The high-tech method is the Litterkwitter (litterkwitter.com.au) which claims to work in just a few weeks with any cat, and comes with instructions and an instructional DVD.

Alternatively you can read the book *How to toilet-train your cat: 21 days to a litter-free home*, by Paul Kunkel, who claims that within three weeks your cat can learn to jump up, perch on the seat, and perform neatly into the bowl, so that you can flush the pee away.

His method is basically to put the litter tray beside the lavatory for a day or two for the cat to use as usual, then to raise the tray an inch on a pile of old magazines. Progressively lift it higher and higher until the litter tray is beside the lavatory seat. Then put it on the seat. Then remove the tray, but cover the top of the pan with plastic sheet and cover that with cat litter, so your cat will think the bowl is a litter tray. Make a small hole in the middle of the plastic; enlarge it day by day, until you can remove the plastic altogether, and your cat will perch on the seat like a person. After all, most cats think they're human! 'Ultimately,' says Mr Kunkel, 'a toilet-trained cat is both happier and healthier, with a gleam in his eye and an extra bounce in his step.' The book is short, folksy, easy to read, full of practical advice and almost convincing.

Most people, however, use some sort of litter tray. Before the advent of today's familiar grey granules, cat boxes were filled with earth, sand, sawdust or ashes – none of which absorbs the liquid or stops the smell nearly as well as the brainchild of Edward Lowe. After WWII he had joined his father's company in Michigan, selling industrial absorbents, including sawdust and Fuller's Earth – kiln-dried clay balls that farmers were showing little enthusiasm for as nesting material. In the winter of 1947, at a cry for help from a neighbour whose pile of sand had frozen solid, whose ashes had given her a house full of sooty pawprints and who thought sawdust might be better, Edward saw another use for his father's Earth.

With this first cat owner a happy convert, he packed the clay into five-pound bags and tried to sell the idea to the local pet-shop – who couldn't see why anyone would pay sixty-five cents to replace dirt-cheap sand. Lowe told him to give the bags away – and the free samples soon earned him a faithful following. His sights set on the wider world, he hawked what he had christened his 'Kitty Litter' – now the generic term in the US – at cat shows, pet shops, and wholesalers – even straight from the boot of his Chevy Coupé. Lowe finally sold his much-refined, dust-controlled, deodorised litter empire in 1990 for many millions of dollars – an empire that would grow and grow thereafter to make many more hundreds of millions annually.

Fuller's Earth is a general term for absorbent clay minerals, capable of taking up their weight in water. It naturally controls some of the smell by soaking up urine, but if urine is left to collect at the bottom of the box, it will soon produce foul-smelling ammonia. Manufacturers now use antibacterial agents to kill the bacteria behind the smell, baking soda to absorb the smell itself, or fragrances simply to mask it.

While this traditional gravel-like form still accounts for forty per cent of the American market, the main rival was developed in the 1980s by Thomas Nelson, a cat-loving biochemist. He investigated several clay compounds, and discovered that various forms of bentonite clump up when they get wet – sodium bentonite most impressively, since sodium ions have a large hydration sphere. Today almost sixty per cent of litter sold in the States is of the clumping sort, most of it made from bentonite clay. The scoopable balls formed when the urine hits the litter can be removed individually, along with dried lumps of faeces, rather than throwing away the whole lot, and the tray topped up – so although clumping litter is more expensive, there is less lugging of the leaden weight of the litter to be done, and not much long-term difference in cost.

Innovation breeds anxiety as well as ease – anxiety (as yet uncorroborated by scientific evidence, and vehemently denied by manufacturers) that the super-absorbent litters might lead to dehydration or intestinal blockage in cats who lick themselves after peeing, or eat the curious litter itself (in purely exploratory spirit, or as an example of pica, a craving for a non-food substance). This anxiety has bred more innovation. There is now a myriad of 'natural' alternatives, made of newspaper or toilet paper, wood pulp, corn cobs, wheat, soy beans, peanut shells and orange peel – even bean sprouts. In the wheat-based varieties, for example, the wheat enzymes neutralise the urine's smell, and its starches trap moisture and clump firmly, for ease of scooping. It and its plant-derived fellows also have the advantage of being lighter and biodegradable – they can be used as mulch, or even flushed down the toilet, doing a little to lighten the load of the landfill sites that swell with an estimated 160,000 tonnes of American cat litter every year.

Another of litter's mixed blessings is the perfume which is added to hide the smell but which risks not only repelling the cat but also lulling its owner into laziness – thus creating a concoction doubly off-putting to the cat's delicate sense of smell and its urge to cleanliness.

And even 'clumpability' has its downside: 'tracking'. Granules stick to a cat's paws and are tracked around the house, leaving the owner to choose between more vacuuming and more scooping. More lateral solutions – such as a screen or grid for the cat to walk across, with a collection tray underneath – only compound complication with complication.

On the other hand, the litter that detects feline lower urinary tract disease by changing colour according to the pH levels of the urine; the box that drains urine past a non-absorbent litter of wax pellets into a removable reservoir, for the particular benefit of diabetic-cat owners who collect samples for testing; and the self-cleaning boxes with patented litter-sifting systems, have all found comfortable urinary niches in the pet-products market. And the products have generated more pets – for once the cat no longer had to be put out for the night for fear of its pee and the pong, it became more like a member of the household – which could now be a smart inner-city cat-flap-less flat.

Dogs

an hound, Whan he comth by the roser or by othere [bushes], though he may nat pisse, yet wole he heve up his leg and make a contenaunce to pisse. (Chaucer, *The Parson's Tale*, ll.857)

The standard dog loo – designed for faeces – is no use in the fight against what some horticulturalists have named 'female dog spot disease' – the round 'burn' spots on lawns where dogs pee. Urban myths have grown here, as in all such fertile trouble spots: namely that female dog urine is more acidic and therefore more damaging than male; and that feeding a dog tomato juice or baking soda makes things magically better.

The problem with urine and faeces on the grass (in smaller quantities a blessing) is their nitrogen content, the result of protein breakdown – and carnivores, including cats and dogs, have quite high-protein diets. What makes urine the major culprit is that it acts all at once as an intense liquid fertilizer, whereas faeces release the waste products only gradually, and can also be easily scooped up and removed. And what makes females guiltier than males has little to do with chemistry and everything to do with conduct: while young dogs of both sexes squat to urinate, males grow out of it and learn to lift a leg for marking, while most females don't (unlike female foxes – see pages 166–168). They will urinate anywhere on a lawn and usually all at once, so destroying patches of grass rather than, as the male does, only a favourite marking post – such as a shrub or tree trunk – with fertiliser overload.

The place where the piss hits the grass will be a brown spot, often with a green halo, for as the urine is diluted away from the centre it begins to have a fertilising effect. And those who take extra efforts with their lawns will be the worst hit – a patch already sated with manufactured fertilisers will be glutted to an overfed death through the dog's extra offering.

An extreme solution would be to re-sow the lawn, since different grasses are variously susceptible – perennial ryegrass has a great nitrogen thirst, where Kentucky bluegrass keels over after a drop or two. A simpler one would be to train the dog to pee elsewhere, encouraging it by collecting its urine and sprinkling it in the preferred area – but not with too many meaty treats as rewards, since these will up the protein levels for the next pee.

Which leads to a third possibility: cutting down on the nitrogen at its dietary source. Most family dogs are sedentary enough not to need as much protein as standard dog food provides. When we scan the supermarket shelves we tend to think that more protein equals better product, but medium- or low-protein foods are fine for all but the most energetic domestic dogs. Another factor is the quality of the protein. In general, the premium pet foods from pet shops and vets have higher-quality protein, which is more digestible, meaning less of it finds it way into the faeces, and possibly the urine. It has been shown that pH has little or no effect on the urine damage to a lawn, so that the numerous 'anti-lawn-burning treats' on sale as functional snacks to 'reward pets while giving owners added benefits' by reducing acid content are likely only to burn holes in bank balances; while if success stories of acidifying urine with fruit juice or alkalinising it with baking soda are true (and they never include a footnote on the heightened risk of bladder stones), it's probably simply as the result of extra liquid, which lowers the urine concentration.

This, and to a lesser extent the urine volume, is the key to the destruction. Much safer ways to make urine more dilute might be to moisten dried food beforehand, or to swap it for canned food, or to add salt or garlic to either (to make the dog thirstier). The popular home remedy of tomato juice increases both salt and water intake, so the dog drinks more and pees more and more dilutedly – though then the cost of green grass might be a dog with a bad heart. A dog with a bladder infection, though, would serve the lawn- if not the dog-lover's purposes, as it will probably have to pee more urgently and frequently, often no more than a few gently fertilising drops at a time. Alternatively, just get a smaller dog ...

Sixteen

… and Other Animals

Mammals use urine or faeces, or the secretions of specialised scent glands rubbed on to trees or other objects, or a combination of these, to mark territory, declare identity, repel predators and attract mates. The commonest way of scent marking is by peeing on inanimate objects. Rodents dribble urine along their runways, male cats spray it in a fine mist on favourite sites, squirrels pee around trees into whose bark they have earlier gnawed a visual marker and foxes urinate around their empty larders to save wasting time returning to them later. Aggressive marking of territory with urine is often part of displays of dominance amongst dogs, while the submissive player's performance adds the dribbling of urine to other servile acts. In wolf packs the dominant males and females ostentatiously undertake the lion's share of the scent marking along their trails, cocking their legs to do so, while the lowlier members simply squat to make puddles when the urge takes them.

Rites of courtship in many mammals also involve the marking of territory, as well as chasing and fighting. A study of the giant panda – for which, as a solitary creature, olfactory communication is especially important – has found that scent marks from males consist of scent-gland material, while those of females are largely urine. The males leave scent marks in the form of a cocktail of smelly chemicals mixed into a stiff gloop that ensures the smell does not fade away too soon; the female scent mark, left most frequently just before she goes on heat, is a watery mixture of over a hundred such smelly chemicals, most of which evaporate rapidly. This satisfies their differing aims – the male to create perimeter markers which will last long enough for them to make the circuit of their home territories, the female to send a swiftly decaying but up-to-date sexual-status report to eligible males. Males also rub urine on their ears, probably because these black, heat-emitting areas help to release important scent components of urine into the environment.

Goats squirt urine forwards into their beards – and, as well as sniffing lightweight, volatile molecules in from the air, have a special nasal cavity into which heavy molecules are sucked, so that males can sample females' urine, adopting a curious lip-curling expression as they do so. Some deer squirt it on to their undersides, and, along with elk and bison, urinate into a mud bath which they then wallow in to coat themselves in a perfumed mud-pack.

The male musk ox can turn its foreskin inside out to create a 12cm-long tube, with a fringe of urine-soaked hairs encrusted with urinary salts, which he swishes to and fro as part of his posturing rituals, sprinkling the pelmet of hair that hangs down from his underbelly. Camels soak their tails in urine and wave them at other camels.

Female tamarin monkeys on heat flirt by rubbing their tails on the urinary perfumes of their own genitalia, before fluttering the scented pennant before their suitors' noses. Rabbits and red foxes skip these preliminaries and urinate directly on to their prospective partners, the male leaping over the female in ritualised dance and showering her from above with his precious perfume.

House mice urine-mark so copiously as to create for themselves a map that dispenses with vision – a scent-scape in which the nose guides them safely over the bridges and past the precipices of their terrain. They do it so much they create stalagmites where repeated urinations – especially by the dominant males and females – combine with dust to form 3cm-high olfactory obelisks. This is a social landscape, too – house mice bred in captivity and trained to recognise other mice by the smell of their urine can distinguish the scents of those differing by only a single gene, so even in the wild the subtleties must be crystal-clear and complex.

Urine works not only on the nose, but on the ovaries and testes. A young male house mouse growing up in the airspace of an adult male's urinary markings reaches puberty later than it otherwise would, even if it never sets eyes on its elder – whereas the same adult's smell, if he is fit to breed, stimulates a female's reproductive system so that two or three days later she comes on heat. Most dramatically, the arrival of a new male breeding rat, mouse or lemming on the scene is enough to terminate a pregnancy and so usurp the previous mate's position – even shortening the female's menstrual cycle from four weeks to three, to speed up his own ensuing appropriation of her. These effects depend on the male's levels of testosterone, which alters the urine's pheromone content and hence smell – so that there is a potent flow of molecular messages between males and females, within and beyond all these bodies, pulsing through blood into urine, and drifting from urine through air.

A study of the South American degu, distant relative to the guinea pig, has provided a possible urinary explanation to the question of why some rodents such as rats and mice have retained ultraviolet vision, where it has evolved out of all other mammals. The degus mark communal paths and wallowing places generously with urine and faeces, for their own and neighbouring colonies' benefit. Fresh degu urine reflects UV much more strongly than visible light, while dry old urine reflects mostly the latter and very little of the former. Thus the degus' UV-sensitive vision allows them to distinguish between fresh and stale marks through sight as well as smell, and so to determine the current social hotspots. The UV is not dispersed by air movements as olfactory signals are – hence a plausible evolutionary pressure to maintain UV vision, which might be extended to other rodents. The drawback, though, could be that birds of prey which hunt by day also have UV vision, and use it to discriminate active from abandoned rodent trails – as kestrels have been shown to do in hunting voles.

Humans, too, have found ways of profiting from the urinary habits of the animal world. Internet magic can provide you with your very own predator pee, collected from tigers, lions, bears and wolves in zoos and wildlife rehab facilities. Gardeners might sprinkle coyote urine to ward off leaf-greedy deer or raccoons, or fox urine to frighten rabbits, skunks and squirrels – or put down a bowl of animal urine to attract butterflies, to brighten and pollinate the back yard (as might collectors, to lure the winged creatures into their nets). Householders keep rats, mice, moles and voles at bay with bobcat urine, while hunters spray urine of the same species as their prey to mask their own human scent and get closer without detection, or urine of the highest predatory species, like the mountain lion, to trick lesser predators – like wild boar and coyote – into thinking they are the hunted as well as the hunter, and let their human prey get away in safety.

The sport of hound trailing in Cumberland has more recently used aniseed to set the trail, but formerly used a cloth on a string soaked in women's pee.

And, in more altruistically complex interaction with the animal kingdom, there is the BioFence, the strategic depositing of animal urine samples to mimic natural scent marking. Researchers in Botswana are experimenting with this technique in the hope of saving from extinction the African wild dog, which has earned itself endangered status by its instinct to roam widely and thus come into fatal contact with humans. They hope to replicate the 'biological fences' that the dogs erect on their territorial borders, and so give the impression that there is a neighbouring pack whose territory should be respected: protective humans are thereby keeping animals from destructive humans, by pretending all these humans are a competing pack of dogs.

Foxes

Zoologist David Macdonald spent fifteen years, in farmland, mountains and suburbia, tracking and stalking foxes by day and night. His studies formed the pungently evocative content of *Running with the Fox*, probing the nature of the beast behind the folklore and the myth. One of his hand-reared cubs, Niff, gradually became his spy in the world of wild foxes:

Niff's first reaction to a scent mark was totally unexpected. She was ten weeks old then, and we were taking a walk around the meadow at Hamels. Suddenly, the cub began to shriek submissively, and dashing up to a tussock of grass, prostrated herself beside it, her tail lashing frantically, before rolling on her back and squirting little pulses of urine into the air. I guessed that her excitement had been caused by a wild fox's scent on the tussock. So, later, I took a few drops of fox urine from my supply in the deep freeze (collected from captive foxes or the bladders of fresh road casualties) and sprinkled it on a path. Then I walked Niff along the path and, sure enough, she fell into similarly rapturous writhings when she came upon the scent.

In the following weeks, as Niff cultivated more characteristic vulpine inscrutability, she grew out of submitting to scent marks. However, she continued to take the greatest care to sniff out tussocks of grass, molehills, tree stumps and other sites where foxes typically leave token urinations. When five months old, however, there was a dramatic change in her behaviour. Until then, the 9th August, she had always squatted to leave a large puddle of urine, and had done so, seemingly as the urge took her, irrespective of the site and without preliminary sniffing. From that day on, she began to token mark, seeking out visually conspicuous sites to anoint with a few drops of her personal perfume.

Enthusiasm leads Macdonald to create a landscape of the scientific sublime verging on the ridiculous: 'Did the pattern in which token marks were deployed hold some clues as to their function? From the outset, I mapped the locations of every one of Niff's marks. Indeed, I continued to do this with Niff and other hand-reared foxes for the next two years …', until he was poring over 'the case histories of 1,283 token urinations!' And then curiosity leads the spectator to tinker with the world of his subject:

> … How was Niff's reaction to a scent mark affected by its whereabouts, and how did Niff's whereabouts affect her reaction to a scent mark? To answer these questions I sprung a game of olfactory musical chairs on Niff – I dug up and moved her favourite marking sites! This was easier to do than one might think, because these sites were often isolated and clearly defined. For example, there was the place where Niff had swung off the path night after night to token mark a tussock of grass which grew among the leaf litter in Dixieland Wood. On the 24th November, I carefully excised this tussock and, without handling it or otherwise contaminating it with scents, carried it to a new site some 50 metres further down Niff's woodland trail. There, in a flat and featureless stretch of the woodland floor, I planted the tussock. At both old and new sites I did everything I could to disguise my gardening, scattering leaf litter over the scarred soil.
>
> That night, Niff's walk began conventionally, and she had left several dozen tokens before arriving at the place from which I had pilfered her marking site. As if on automatic pilot, she swung off the main path to the spot, three metres

to the side, where she customarily marked. There is no doubt that she was taken aback. She looked around, cast from side to side with her nose, and then, with the vulpine equivalent of a shrug, of her shoulders, continued on her way. Two or three strides later she caught the scent and drew to an abrupt halt and back-tracked cautiously. Doubtless it was my imagination running riot, but her expression seemed to say 'Oh no! Not another experiment!' Of one thing there is no doubt: she doused the transplanted tussock in urine, and emphasized her point with a carefully positioned dropping.

But in the end the riddles remain insoluble: 'The fact remains that we have few good answers to the key question – what messages do scents communicate between foxes? ... Lamenting the noselessness of man, Kenneth Grahame in *Wind in the Willows*, called scents "fairy calls from the void", for which "we have only the word smell, to include the whole range of delicate thrills which murmur in the nose of the animal night and day, summoning, warning, inciting and repelling." Until we can decipher these messages we can scarcely claim to understand fox society.'

Wolves

Farley Mowat's *Never Cry Wolf* is the lupine equivalent of Macdonald's exploration of the fox's world. Mowat was sent by the Canadian Wildlife Service to spend a summer in the Arctic, to investigate complaints that wolves were decimating the deer population of the Canadian wilderness.

Urine is Mowat's means of finally convincing himself of his safety amongst his subjects, through amateurish imitation of them:

> ... One of the facts which had emerged was that they were not nomadic roamers, as is almost universally believed, but were settled beasts and the possessors of a large permanent estate with very definite boundaries ... clearly indicated in wolfish fashion.

> 'nyone who has observed a dog doing his neighborhood rounds and leaving his personal mark on each convenient post will already have guessed how the wolves marked out *their* property. Once a week, more or less, the clan made the rounds of the family lands and freshened up the boundary markers – a sort of lupine beating of the bounds. This careful attention to property rights was perhaps made necessary by the presence of two other wolf families whose lands abutted on ours, although I never discovered any evidence of bickering or disagreement between the owners of the various adjoining estates. I suspect, therefore, that it was more of a ritual activity.

> In any event, once I had become aware of the strong feeling of property rights which existed amongst the wolves, I decided to use this knowledge to make them at least recognise my existence. One evening, after they had gone off for their regular nightly hunt, I staked out a property claim of my own, embracing perhaps three acres, with the tent at the middle, and *including a hundred-yard long section of the wolves' path.*

Staking the land turned out to be rather more difficult than I had anticipated. In order to ensure that my claim would not be overlooked, I felt obliged to make a property mark on stones, clumps of moss, and patches of vegetation at intervals of not more than fifteen feet around the circumference of my claim. This took most of the night and required frequent returns to the tent to consume copious quantities of tea; but before dawn had brought the hunters home the task was done, and I retired, somewhat exhausted, to observe results.

I had not long to wait. At 0814 hours, according to my wolf log, the leading male of the clan appeared over the ridge behind me, padding homeward with his usual air of preoccupation. As usual he did not deign to glance at the tent; but when he reached the point where my property line intersected the trail, he stopped as abruptly as if he had run into an invisible wall. He was only fifty yards from me and with my binoculars I could see his expression very clearly.

His attitude of fatigue vanished and was replaced by a look of bewilderment. Cautiously he extended his nose and sniffed at one of my marked bushes. He did not seem to know what to make of it or what to do about it. After a minute of complete indecision he backed away a few yards and sat down. And then, finally, he looked directly at the tent and at me. It was a long, thoughtful, considering sort of look.

Having achieved my object – that of forcing at least one of the wolves to take cognizance of my existence – I now began to wonder if, in my ignorance, I had transgressed some unknown wolf law of major importance and would have to pay for my temerity. I found myself regretting the absence of a weapon as the look I was getting became longer, yet more thoughtful, and still more intent.

I began to grow decidedly fidgety, for I dislike staring matches, and in this particular case I was up against a master, whose yellow glare seemed to become more baleful as I attempted to stare him down.

The situation was becoming intolerable. In an effort to break the impasse I loudly cleared my throat and turned my back on the wolf (for a tenth of a second) to indicate as clearly as possible that I found his continued scrutiny impolite, if not actually offensive.

He appeared to take the hint. Getting to his feet he had another sniff at my marker, and then he seemed to make up his mind. Briskly, and with an air of decision, he turned his attention away from me and began a systematic tour of the area I had staked out as my own. As he came to each boundary marker he sniffed it once or twice, then carefully placed his mark on the outside of each clump of grass or stone. As I watched I saw where I, in my ignorance, had erred. He made his mark with such economy that he was able to complete the entire circuit without having to reload once, or, to change the simile slightly, he did it all on one tank of fuel.

The task completed – and it had taken him no longer than fifteen minutes – he rejoined the path at the point where it left my property and trotted off towards his home – leaving me with a good deal to occupy my thoughts.

Once it had been formally established and its existence ratified by the wolves themselves, my little enclave in their territory remained inviolate. Never again did a wolf trespass on my domain. Occasionally, one in passing would stop to freshen up some of boundary marks on his side of the line, and, not to be outdone in ceremony, I followed suit to the best of my ability. Any lingering doubts I might have had as to my personal safety dissolved, and I was free to devote all my attention to the study of the beasts themselves.

Horses

In a sanitised take on age-old urine-drinking practices, the messy quaffing of the liquid can now be bypassed and its valuable ingredients distilled out into immaculate and unobjectionable pill form. Following on from a long Chinese tradition of prescribing concentrated distillates of hormones from urine for problems with menstruation, pregnancy and sex, horse urine is now a major source of the hormones used to make HRT drugs for menopausal women – 22 million women worldwide, and demand is growing.

Pregnant mares' urine (PMU), high in oestrogen, has been found effective in creating drugs to treat depression, heart disease, osteoporosis and infertility, and it may even combat some forms of cancer. PMU farming is a multi-billion-dollar North American industry. Attempts to widen the field to Australia have in the past been countered by animal-welfare concerns, and although some still declare the entire industry inhumane, an Australian company has adapted the traditional horse nappy, originally designed to keep dung off the stable floor, into a urine collector; and the horses have apparently adapted well to their new accessory. This bridge between the agricultural and pharmaceutical industries has been nationally funded, as prototype after costly prototype edged closer to solving the problem of how to prevent contamination of the urine by the faeces, since faeces kill the oestrogens. Computer modelling and medical, veterinary and physiotherapeutic expertise finally found the elusive grail: a pliable, medical-grade silicone shield. The horses wear the 'device' from four o'clock in the afternoon till eight o'clock the next morning, during which period an estimated ninety-two per cent of the urine they pass is caught, adding up to about eight litres a day. They are brought in at tea-time, a rug placed on their back and a bladder-bag clipped on under their stomach; then comes the collecting device itself, plugged in underneath. And so, clad in their new pyjamas, they proceed back out to the paddock.

By contrast, the American system, in which a hundred thousand horses across the country are confined in tiny stalls with a catheter in the bladder, barely able to move, in

a state of constant dehydration in order that they produce concentrated urine, and all the while carrying the foal which is at the natural centre of all this hormonal production and profit, is compared by animal-welfare groups to battery-hen farming. So oestrogen from these new Antipodean PMU farms is the equivalent of the free-range egg, as the horses can roam freely, are fed native grains to promote production of the best oestrogens, and don't have their foals sold off at three months as do their artificially impregnated American sisters. Rather than the foals being an inconvenient by-product, often sent off to slaughter and the dog-food factory, their working mothers are granted maternity leave from the production line to bring them up, and the foals themselves are seen as a positive step towards breeding an elite of both working horses and thoroughbreds – a great radiation of productive spokes with urine as its hub.

Extensive stress tests, checking daily for signs such as attempts to avoid the device, changes in grazing or social behaviour, in heart rate and hormonal levels, an increase in injuries, have given vets and scientists confidence that these techniques might soon be setting the world standard – not least because the ethics seem to pay off. Techniques have been painstakingly developed to reduce the litres of urine down to grams of hormonal gold-dust, as distilled powder or gel, to be sent to the States for 'fingerprinting' – stringent comparison against the American best. And it might even be better than the 'real thing'; a happy horse, it seems, is awash with high-quality hormones.

Concerns haven't been only for the horses, though. Recent scares that HRT (in this case, a combination of horse oestrogens and progestin, a synthetic form of progesterone) may increase the risk of breast cancer, heart attack and stroke have been consolidated by some doctors, with the suggestion that both agricultural collection and synthetic creation are cheap and easy evasions of the fact that neither of their products belongs in the human body, but rather in the horse or chemical factory it came from. The principal horse oestrogen is the ultra-high-strength 'equilin', with a molecular structure different to any found in humans. It may be 'natural', but nature's seas are wider and less well-charted than some merchants of its bounty would have us believe. Nonetheless, the evidence is far from clear-cut, and meanwhile the slightly less cheap and more humanely cheerful version of PMU farming proceeds apace. This strange pharmaceutical industry might yet be further milked by bringing cows to join the mares. Pregnant cows, too, have a very high percentage of conjugated oestrogen in their urine, and although beef cattle appear the most suitable, it may end up being the dairy farmers, struggling after deregulation of the Australian milk market, who promote their herds most forcefully as the biotechnological golden-milk-cows of the future.

Porcupines

There is a delightful myth that the courting male porcupine pees on his beloved in order to soften her prickly defences before mounting her. Sadly, this proves to be only a half-truth. The piss is more a simple scented shower than a functional quill-softener, an imperious olfactory added-extra to the foreplay rather than a physically essential lubricant. One study of the animals describes how, as the mating season approaches, the male begins to show increased interest in the places where the female has urinated; and how, several times in the last weeks and days before copulation, he smells the female all over, then rears up on his hind legs, his penis fully erect. If the female is not ready, she runs away; if she is, she mirrors his pose and they stand belly-to-belly. It is now that the male, in most cases, sprays the female with a long copious stream of urine (once in the survey reaching a distance of over six feet from the point of discharge), drenching her from head to foot. Depending on her physical readiness (or opinion of her suitor) the female makes her distaste known with a variable degree of abruptness: she either objects vocally, or strikes out with her front paws like a boxer, or threatens or tries to bite – or just shakes off the urine and runs away.

The elders of the Alaskan Yup'ik Eskimos, at the 1983 Bristol Bay Native Convention, expressed for the benefit of the younger generation their core human values, and uttered in addition words of more practical advice – amongst which figured: porcupine urine, as an unrivalled salve for aches, pains and arthritis (human children's urine, sometimes mixed with seal oil for energy, should be drunk to combat hypothermia; or any old urine rubbed on the body after working up a heavy sweat by dancing, to make an oily lather before plunging into the river and washing it all off in an icily cleansing bath).

Bears

Unlike the suspended animation of some smaller mammals, bear hibernation, also called winter sleep, is not so cold or deep. Heart rate, body temperature and oxygen use all drop; and defecation and urination cease, to prevent dehydration. The sleepers live off their own body fat, producing a minimum of waste – just water and carbon dioxide; and they recycle what urine they do produce, converting toxic urea into usable protein – a feat which scientists hope to translate into help for sufferers of kidney disease.

Butterflies

Butterflies do most of their eating before birth, as it were. The lowly caterpillar spends its days scoffing so that the ethereal butterfly can emerge from the chrysalis fully-formed. But despite having done the bulk of the intake in larval form, the butterfly still needs to top up its supply of nutrients for its few days of life. And this it likes to do by drinking urine. Anyone's will do: they'll sup from puddles of any animal piss, or lick from leaves soaked in it by uncoiling their proboscis (a trunk-like sucking apparatus) and laying it along the edge of a water droplet, drawing the liquid up through this tubular tongue. Humans can even buy bottles of the stuff, inventively packaged – a great pure product from a renewable source – to pour into a bowl and attract butterflies as water baths do birds. The minerals, vitamins and sodium in urine are what attract them, along with the nitrogen which is found also in some of their other favourites, rotting fruit and meat, or dung; while from nectar, pollen and tree sap they take the sugar to give them strength to fly.

Reindeer and Mushrooms

European and Russian explorers began in the mid-seventeenth century to bring back tales of life in the Siberian wastes. They reported how for many Siberian reindeer-herding tribes, such as the Koryak and the Chukchi, the *Amanita muscaria*, or fly-agaric, mushroom was a central sacred part of their shamanic practices; and that reindeer were equally sacred animals, being a source of food, shelter, clothing – and an indirect path back to the primary sacred object. Although the mushrooms, one of which was worth three reindeer, were sometimes dried, or made into a soup or liqueur for a gentler hit, they were usually simply shredded and chewed with water, or rolled into small pellets and swallowed – triggering first invigoration, then hallucination, finally unconsciousness as the mushroom spirits drew the eater away from this world and into another.

Reindeer have as much a taste for all this as humans do, although from the outside, when they indulge, all they look is stupefied and tottery. But their other weakness, especially after dining on certain mosses and lichens, is a chaser of urine, their own or that of humans – so much so that Russian anthropologist Waldemar Jochelson reported in 1905 that men urinating in the open ran the risk of unleashing an eager reindeer stampede from all quarters – pee-stained snow is a particular delicacy. The animals' taste for piss may also have had the more prosaic explanation of being a means of conserving salts such as nitrates, which were in short supply in their diet. But the predilection was effectively exploited in a variation on the BioFence, not to keep reindeer away, but – by collecting the animals' urine in sealskin vessels which they called 'the reindeer's night-chamber' – to attract those who persisted in standing aloof from the herd.

The reindeer's penchant for pee may also have been what gave the tribesmen their own inspiration. Human urine could be recycled, with fitting druggy democracy, for a second-hand (indeed, up to fifth- or sixth-hand) magic-mushroom experience. Around eighty-five per cent of the fungi's major psychoactive compound (ibotenic acid) is not metabolised by the body into the psychoactive molecule (muscimole), but remains intact and active in its passage through the kidneys and bladder, so that the urine contains five or six times as much of the drug as a single body can assimilate, which means there is plenty to spare for the next drinker. The Koryaks know this by experience, and the urine of persons intoxicated with fly agaric is not wasted. 'The drinker himself drinks it to prolong the state of hallucination, or offers it to others as a treat,' Jochelson observed.

Filip Johann von Strahlenberg, a Swedish prisoner of war in the early eighteenth century, reported seeing lesser Koryak tribespeople loitering greedily outside huts where the trips were in full swing, waiting for the door to open and their outstretched wooden bowls to be filled with the hot golden ambrosia of their betters. This seemingly inferior route to the high was in fact a safer one (and less likely to end in the vomiting that is the usual side-effect), since many of the toxic compounds are processed and eliminated by the first body they travel through.

Victorian travellers, too, returned with heady tales of fungus and piss, amongst them the mycologist Mordecai Cooke, who mentions the recycling of urine rich in the active agent muscimol in his *A Plain and Easy Account of British Fungi* of 1862; he was, incidentally, a friend of Charles Dodgson (Lewis Carroll), who may have transposed Cooke's reports of the characteristic effect of macropsia (the inability to judge size) into Alice's tentative eating of the mushroom, one half of which makes her grow very tall, the other very small – 'And now which is which?' ...

This plethora of reciprocal piss-drinking is at the heart of the archaic motif of the shaman in deer-antlered headgear and deer-skin robe, and has been claimed to be the origin of the phrase 'to get pissed', preceding alcoholic intoxication by thousands of years (and finally brought to an end in Siberia by alcohol itself, introduced by the Russians on their sixteenth- and seventeeth-century conquests). Another cultural offshoot might have been the Christmas myths of flying reindeer and their euphorically chuckling, ruddily flushed master – size distortion and flying are at the heart of many of the hallucinations, and the mushroom harvesters wore red fur-trimmed coats and big black boots, came carrying sacks with their spoils, and entered and left by the birch pole that supported the smoke holes of their huts.

Mushroom-eaters today still preach the wisdom of the same water-stewed recipe that von Strahlenberg recorded: steep over the oven's lowest heat setting for one hour to create a tea; drink two cups and then proceed to consume urine; after first passing water wait an hour before consuming any more source material; do not waste your urine – keep recycling until you achieve the proper effects ... The only concession to squeamish modernity is the tip to mix the piss with lemonade, or perhaps to wash it down with an iced tea chaser.

Bibliography and Other Sources

Brewer's Dictionary of Phrase & Fable, Sixteenth Edition,
   revised by Adrian Room (Cassell, London, 2001)
The Oxford Dictionary of Quotations, Third Edition (Oxford
   University Press, 1980)
The Penguin Dictionary of Modern Quotations, J.M. & M.J.
   Cohen (Penguin, London, 1971)
The Wordsworth Book of Euphemism, Judith S. Neaman
   & Carole G. Silver (Wordsworth Editions Ltd, Ware,
   Hertfordshire, 1983) – originally published as *Kind words:
   a thesaurus of euphemisms* (Facts on File, Inc., New York)

Baker, Nicholson, *The Mezzanine* (Granta Books,
   Cambridge, 1986)
Bhikkhu, Thanissaro, *The Buddhist Monastic Code Volume
   II: The Khandhaka Rules Translated & Explained* (tr.
   Geoffrey DeGraff, 2002) (www.accesstoinsight.org/lib/
   authors/thanissaro/bmc2/index.html)
Boire, Richard Glen, *Dangerous Lessons* (www.cognitiveliberty.
   org/news/dangerous_lessons.htm
Chapman, Christopher, *piss art: Images of Urination in 20th
   century art* (http://.ensemble.va.com.au)

Chaucer, Geoffrey, *The Canterbury Tales* (ed. F N Robinson, Oxford University Press, London, 1957)

Chevallier, Gabriel, *Clochemerle* (tr. Jocelyn Godefroi, Martin Secker & Warburg, 1936)

Cooke, Mordecai, *A Plain and Easy Account of British Fungi* (Robert Hardwicke, London, 1862)

Crowley, Mike, 'When Gods Drank Urine' *Fortean Studies*, vol. III, 1996

Devereux, Paul, *Urine Luck: The Amanita Story*, www.lightworks.com

Ellis, Havelock, *Studies in the psychology of sex* (7 volumes, 1897–1928)

Eno, Brian, *A Year With Swollen Appendices* (Faber & Faber, London, 1996)

Etshalom, Rabbi Yitzchok, *Hilkhot K'riat Sh'ma (Laws of Reading the Sh'ma)*, *Kriat Shema 3:6–9*, www.torah.org

Freud, Sigmund, *Civilization and its Discontents* (tr. and ed. James Strachey, W. W. Norton, New York, 1961)

Gardner, Martin, 'Urine Therapy', *Skeptical Inquirer*, May–June 1999

Gold, Gary 'Pig', 'The Rolling Stones: 109 Reasons Why the Rolling Stones were the World's Greatest Rock and Roll Band' (www.inmusicwetrust.com/articles/54f03.html)

Graham-Rowe, Duncan, 'Army rations rehydrated by urine', *New Scientist*, 21.7.2004

Grass, Günter, *Die Blechtrommel* (*The Tin Drum*, tr. Ralph Manheim, Martin Secker & Warburg, 1962)

Hart-Davis, Adam, *Thunder, Flush, and Thomas Crapper* (Michael O'Mara Books Ltd, London, 1997)

Irving, John, *The Water-Method Man* (Black Swan, London, 1986)

Joyce, James, *Ulysses* (Paris, 1922)

Khomeini, R; Reuh Alleah Khumaynei, *The Little Green Book: Sayings of Ayatollah Khomeini, Political, Philosophical, Social and Religious* (tr. H. Salemson, Bantam Books, New York, 1985)

Kunkel, Paul, *How to toilet-train your cat: 21 days to a litter-free home* (Workman Publishing, New York, 1991)

Lee, Tim, 'Benefits of horse urine', *Landline*, 2.6.2002 (www. abc.net.au/landline)

Lémery, Nicolaus, *Dictionnaire universel des drogues simples* (Paris, 1759)

Lewis, Justin, *Tastiest Torah Treats* (www.kolel.org)

Lupton, Thomas, *A thousand notable things of sundry sortes whereof some are wonderfull, some straunge, some pleasant, divers necessary, a great sort profitable, and many very precious* (London, 1579)

Macdonald, David, *Running with the Fox* (Unwin Hyman, London, 1987)

Marshall, Leon, 'Wild Dog Urine May Be Used as 'Fences' in Africa', *National Geographic News*, 3.11.2004

Mowat, Farley, *Never Cry Wolf* (Ballantine Books, London, 1963)

Rabelais, François, *Five books of the lives, heroic deeds and sayings of Gargantua and his son Pantagruel* (tr. Sir Thomas Urquhart of Cromarty – Books I & II, 1653; Book III, 1693 – & Peter Antony Motteux – Books IV & V, 1708, Globusz Publishing, New York, Berlin, 2002: www.globusz.com/ebooks/rabelais/00000001.htm)

Root-Bernstein, Robert & Michèle, *Honey, Mud, Maggots, and Other Medical Marvels: The Science Behind Folk Remedies and Old Wives' Tales* (Pan Books, London, 2000)

Shakespeare, William, *The Complete Works* (Collins, London & Glasgow, 1951)

Spector, Jack, 'Duchamp's Gendered Plumbing: A Family Business?', *tout-fait*: The Marcel Duchamp Studies Online Journal (Perpetual, 2005, www.toutfait.com/duchamp.jsp?posyid=3600&keyword=)

Stead, Jennifer, with assistance from Arthur Saul, 'The Uses of Urine', *Old West Riding*, vol. 1 no. 2, Spring 1982

van der Kroon, Coen, *The Golden Fountain: The Complete Guide to Urine Therapy* (Wishland Publishing, Scottsdale, Arizona, 1996)

Wasson, R Gordon, *SOMA: The Divine Mushroom of Immortality* (Harcourt Brace Jovanovich, New York, 1968)

Weinberg, Jonathan, 'Urination and its Discontents', *Journal of Homosexuality*, vol. 27 issue 1/2, 1994

Adam McLean's Alchemy Website www.levity.com (including *Names of the Philosophers' Stone*, collected by William Gratacolle)

www.arts.ualberta.ca

http://creativeproverbs.com

www.etymonline.com

www.everything2.com

www.globusz.com

www.halfbakery.com

www.imdb.com

www.jokes.com

www.newscientist.com
www.nlm.nih.gov/medlineplus/ency (MedlinePlus Medical
    Encyclopedia)
www.peevish.co.uk/slang
www.rotten.com
http://skepdic.com (The Skeptic's Dictionary)
www.slangsite.com
www.snopes.com (urban legends)
www.wikipedia.org

Index